Trail of Thread

A Woman's Westward Journey

Trail of Thread

A Woman's Westward Journey

Linda K. Hubalek

Butterfield Books Inc.
Lindsborg, Kansas

Trail of Thread
© 1995 by Linda K. Hubalek
Eighth Printing 2002
Printed in the United States of America

For details and order blanks for the *Butter in the Well* Series, the *Trail of Thread* Series, and the *Planting Dreams* Series, please see page 110 in the back of this book. If you wish to contact the publisher or author, please address to Butterfield Books, Inc., PO Box 407, Lindsborg, KS 67456-0407. Each book is $9.95, plus $3.00 s/h for the first book ordered and $.50 for each additional book.

Consulting Editor: Dianne Russell
Cover Design: Jody Chapel, Cover to Cover Design
Cover photo courtesy of Kansas State Historical Society
Maps courtesy of Linda K. Hubalek
Quilt design used on cover: Sawtooth star

Publisher's Cataloging in Publication
  (Prepared by Quality Books Inc.)

Hubalek, Linda K.
Trail of thread : a woman's westward journey / Linda K. Hubalek.
-- Aurora, Colo. : Butterfield Books, 1995.
p. cm. -- (Trail of Thread ; 1)
Includes bibliographical references.
SUMMARY : Letters recreate a family's wagon trail walk from Kentucky to Kansas in 1854.
Audience: Age: 9-18.
Preassigned LCCN: 95-78434.
ISBN 1-886652-06-6.
1. --Frontier and pioneer life--Juvenile fiction. 2. West (U.S.)--History --Juvenile fiction. I. Title.
PZ7.H833Tra 1995   813'.54
                        QB195-20370

To the women who walked the trail.

I hope you realized your journeys were not in vain.

Books by Linda K. Hubalek

Butter in the Well
Prärieblomman
Egg Gravy
Looking Back
Trail of Thread
Thimble of Soil
Stitch of Courage
Planting Dreams
Cultivating Hope
Harvesting Faith

Acknowledgments

I would like to express my sincerest thanks to all of the people who helped with the *Trail of Thread*, especially my research team, Ivan Pieratt, Ione Johnson, and Leland Akers. I enjoyed retracing the trail with you. Thank you very much for your time and devotion to the project.

Linda Katherine Johnson Hubalek

Table of Contents

Trail of Thread ix
Leaving Home 1
Hot Wax and Tears 17
Pickles Downstream 33
Doctoring with Whiskey 49
Warm Milk and Mud 63
Jumping the Gun 91
Quilt Patterns 100
Family Chart 101
Map of Route 102
Bibliography 105

Map of Kansas and Nebraska-1854

Trail of Thread

When I started research for the *Trail of Thread* series, my goal was to show what life was like for the thousands of women who had to prepare their families for a cross-country journey into the unknown. What were the feelings of these women when they were told they were going to move into an open wilderness without family or towns nearby? How could they decide what to pack and what they must leave behind? Most women were traveling during their childbearing years and had pregnancies and several young children to take care of on the way. What were their worries and concerns?

Digging into my ancestors' pasts, I found not only their trail paths but also documents that connected their lives to important happenings that shaped the course of American history. They were ordinary people—from the North and the South—but looking back at their lives, I see they played important roles in making our nation what it is today.

The women moved to the new territory because they dreamed of rich farmland and peaceful communities for their children. Instead, these women of varying backgrounds had to come together to form a patchwork of unity in order to survive the uncertainty and stress of the times. Little did they know when they left their homes and staked new claims in the territory of Kansas that their families and land would be involved in the clashes of the free-state versus proslavery forces, which plunged the nation into the Civil War. The women were caught in the middle, having to take care of family and homestead while the men were away from home defending their country's battle lines.

Deborah Goodpaster Pieratt, my great-great-great grand-mother, and the main character of the first book in the *Trail of*

Thread series, traveled from Kentucky to Kansas in 1854. In this first book, written in the form of letters, Deborah describes the scenery, everyday events on the trail, and the task of taking care of her six young children. Through her words, you learn what it was like for the families who pulled up stakes and ventured past civilization into unsettled territory. Her immediate goal was the preservation of her family against the perils of the road—accidents, sickness, robbery, homesickness, and boredom. Death, and the possibility that the family would fail to find what they were looking for, were constantly in the back of her mind.

Unfortunately, hints of trouble ahead plagued them along the way as people questioned their motive for settling in the new territory. Though Deborah didn't realize it, her letters show how this trip affected her family for generations to come.

The second book portrays the widowed Margaret Ralston Kennedy—from the North—who brings her eight children and their families to Kansas in 1855. Settling near the Pieratts, they form friendships and businesses, all the while fighting the conflicts that are tearing the territory apart.

In the third book, Mrs. Kennedy's niece, Maggie, orphaned at age three in Ohio, eventually follows her family to Kansas and marries Deborah Pieratt's son, James. The country is now gripped by the Civil War, which affects the union between the two families.

To be as accurate as possible in my writing, I have stood on the home places they left behind, traveled the trails they would have taken, viewed the rivers and streams they crossed, felt the same April air, and sensed the magnitude of their adventure. The trails have evolved into roads and towns over the years, but the scenery—and the sense of isolation—have not changed at all in some areas since the 1850s. And at the end of the journey, I stood on the land in Kansas where their trails ended.

Now it's your turn to travel the *Trail of Thread*.

Leaving Home

I heard the men's low voices mixed in with childish laughter as I carefully descended the steps, balancing a tray of food on my shoulder. My widowed mother-in-law, Sarah, runs a road-house for travelers in the basement of her log home. The stage-coach stops by regularly, as do cattle traders on foot. She serves the travelers food and the area's best whiskey, and puts them up for the night. I am helping out tonight because, besides her customers, her sons John (my husband) and James and our two families are here visiting this Tuesday evening. A third brother, David, and his family live with Sarah and help out with the inn and the farming. All were gathered in the basement room for the evening meal. My oldest five, James's four, and David's three children played noisily around the room, chasing one another in and out of the shadows cast by the few candles. The earthen floor muffled the sounds' vibration off the rough stone walls. We also each have young babies, who were somehow sleeping peacefully together on a side cot in the noisy room.

John, David, and James were grilling a lone traveler about something, oblivious to the rampages of their children. If the poor man was hoping for a refreshing meal and a peaceful night's rest, he picked the wrong inn tonight. He should be thankful Sarah's other four children aren't here with their families, too.

I usually don't pay attention when the men talk about politics, but I automatically listened while I laid the dishes of food

1

in front of them. They were discussing the new government bill that proposes to open up prairie Indian land, west of Missouri, to white settlement. A bill called the Territory of Platte failed last spring due to Southern opposition. Now an amended bill, breaking up the land into two sections, the Territory of Nebraska and the Territory of Kansas, is being discussed. Problems of slavery being legal in the new territories are being hotly debated between the Northern and Southern states. It sounds like the government has determined that the people who settle the territories can decide whether they want to allow slavery in their new states.

The traveler carefully pulled a folded newspaper clipping out of his front jacket pocket and handed it to John. Holding it up to the candlelight, John read out loud that when the bill passes in the spring, as they predict it will, a man can claim whatever land he wants in these new territories for about a dollar an acre.

Kentucky was a wilderness in the early 1800s, when John's grandfather, Valentine Pieratt, moved his family here from Maryland. He sailed across the sea in 1780 from France to fight in the Revolutionary War, decided to stay in the New World, and moved westward to new wilderness whenever the area he lived in became populated.

Because land is getting scarce here for new generations, the idea of plenty of cheap land immediately stirred our men's interest. I believe the adventure of their grandfather haunts their thinking, too.

When John finished reading that article and looked up into my eyes, I knew his mind was set to move as soon as possible. He wanted to blaze his own trail to the new territory and be ready to stake his claim when the land opened up. We are partners in life, but I knew I had no say in this move.

Today is my thirty-third birthday. Where will I be on the next? Will my children survive the trip and be around me to help celebrate it?

January 28, 1854

A day later—by strange fate—James and Mary got a letter from Mary's brother, Albert Tipton, in Missouri. He plans to move from Boone County, Missouri, to the new territory in Kansas this spring. Was anyone back in Kentucky game to start a new family colony with him?

Debates, calculating, and reservations finally gave way to the decision that would affect the families, going on the trip and staying behind. We're leaving for the Kansas Territory in two short months.

Our families, the Pieratts, Goodpasters, and Tiptons, have intermarried with each new generation born in Kentucky. I hate to leave such a tight clan and head off by ourselves. Of my five older Goodpaster brothers—two married two of John's sisters— none wanted to uproot their families.

Ann, my younger sister, who has lived with us the past few years, decided to stick with our family and travel with us. We've heard that a change of climate can improve a person's health, so we urged her to come along. Ann has always been on the frail side, with weak lungs, so I hope the trip will mend her condition.

My three younger half-brothers live with my widowed stepmother, Betsy, who is also John's aunt. Twenty-two years older than I, she has been our "mother" and big sister since I was five years old and Ann was two. Betsy is the one person I am going to miss the most when we leave Kentucky.

Both James and David Pieratt married Tiptons, and so did their sister, Eva Lou. All these Tipton families contemplated the trip since their brothers, Samuel and Albert, and their families, moved to Missouri several years ago. So far only James and Mary have decided to join us.

March 14, 1854

After weeks of preparation, we start on the road tomorrow. If I had my way, we would stay put, but I reminded myself constantly as we packed that we're moving for the opportunity it will give our children. My concern is the danger of the journey and the hardships we may meet in the new land. There is no guarantee that life will be better for us in Kansas Territory.

We debated, but finally packed two wagons for each family. We felt it was better for the animals' sake to limit the weight on each wagon to around 2000 pounds instead of overloading one wagon. Since we aren't going all the way to California, we figured we could stand the cost of two wagons. Because we're moving to a wilderness, we tried to pack what we can't do without. I imagine we'll go by town stores and trading posts near the Missouri-Kansas line, but I suspect everything will cost outrageously more on the edge of the frontier. And why buy it when we already own that item?

Since we need six oxen per wagon, we bought extra animals a few weeks ago. John decided to use oxen instead of mules because the oxen are easily managed, patient, and gentle—even with the children—and not easily driven off or prone to stampeding like mules or horses. John hitched the new pairs to the middle of the teams and drove them around the yard to get them used to one another. Time and distance will get them into the routine. After we arrive at our destination, the extra oxen we bought for the trip will be sold to others going farther than Kansas, or they'll be eaten this winter.

Between the two families, we will have the extra oxen, four horses, eight mules, ten cows, and a bull in our traveling herd.

I would have loved to bring a couple of sows along, but I'm afraid the only pork we will have is smoked and salted. We'll have to find a farmer closer to where we settle to restock our swine herd. Here we have a large herd that roam the hills and valleys of the Pieratt lands. They eat acorns in the woods and fatten up real nice. The pigs are butchered for the food needed at the roadhouse and also for the whole Pieratt-Goodpaster winter supply of meat.

After much discussion, John agreed to hitch a cage of chickens on the back of a wagon. I thought about trying to pack eggs in the flour sacks, but I was afraid they would break and spoil the flour. After a few days on the trail, I hope the chickens settle down and produce eggs for us. Many recipes are hard to fix

4

without them. If they don't lay, we'll have stewed chicken along the way.

Yesterday we sold everything that wouldn't fit in the wagons at a public auction on our farm. The strain of the day is still on my mind. This morning I've been ready to fetch something and then I stop in midstep, wondering if it's tucked in the wagon or if it was sold yesterday. It was hard to see most of the animals and all but a few chickens leave the place. But we can't take everything along, and we need the money.

John rebuilt two farm wagons for the trip. The running gear from the wagons, which controls the wheels and steering mechanism, were reinforced, and a forged iron rod was attached along the length of the wagon tongues to strengthen them. Three wheels were rebuilt and all were soaked to tighten the wood to the rims. An extra bow, open links to repair chains, bolts, ropes, and so on are packed for repairs to the wagons if we need them.

New wagon beds were built using seasoned oak boards. Sides were jointed together. No nails were used that could work out along the bumpy trial and spell disaster. Along the inside of the three-foot-high sides, John built long boxes running the length of the wagon for storage. These boxes will serve as seats during the day if the children want to ride inside. We just add boards cut to fit across the storage boxes, put bedding on top, and the wagon is outfitted for sleeping. The boards fit in a wooden holder that runs along the outside of the wagon. They can also be used to make a bench or table when laid across stumps or, heaven forbid, as lumber for a coffin.

I had a big hand in preparing the wagons, too. The wagon beds were outfitted with a framework of hickory bows high enough to give a head clearance, and I hand-sewed long pieces of cloth together for coverings. It was quite an undertaking. It had to be tight, strong enough to withstand heavy winds, and rainproof so the things inside don't get soaked. Even though it was extra work, I ended up making them a double thickness of cloth to keep out the cold. A dark muslin went over the framework first, then a heavy white linen. The dark cloth helps cut down on the brightness of the reflection as we walk beside the wagon. I coated the outside material with a mixture of hot beeswax and

5

linseed oil for waterproofing. It turned the material a sand color, which should help the reflection, too. The covering is drawn together on the ends by a strong cord to form tight circles. End flaps can be buttoned on to completely seal the wagon top. My stitches and buttonholes will be tested by the first storm we run into. I even stitched pockets on the inside of the covering to hold little things like our comb, sunbonnets, and other personal things I didn't want packed out of reach.

The first wagon holds all our provisions, like food, utensils, and clothing that we'll need every day.

It was tough to decide how much food we should bring along. How many times this past week have I gone down to the cellar, pulled something off the shelf to pack in the wagon, and then stood there trying to decide if it's the right thing to bring along? I've agonized over every little thing as the wagon started to fill up. How long will we be on the road? Will we be on our land early enough to plant crops and a garden this spring, or do we need to bring enough to last us through the winter? Will there be farmers or towns nearby where we can buy food if we run out? Questions like these have plagued me since the decision was made.

John borrowed a guidebook to Oregon and California from a neighbor,which suggested that for each adult going to California, a party should carry two hundred pounds of flour, thirty of hardtack, seventy-five of bacon, ten of rice, five of coffee, two of tea, twenty-five of sugar, two of saleratus, ten of salt, a half-bushel each of cornmeal, parched, and ground corn, and a small keg of vinegar. We're not going on to California (unless the men change their minds), so we shouldn't need that much per person, but we'll need supplies until we get crops and garden planted and harvested. Who knows how long it will be until towns with stores get established in the new territory?

Even though it would be hard work to do, the best way to bring food along for the trip would be to haul everything I have in the food cellar up and pack it in the wagon. Unfortunately, not everything would fit, crocks may break jostling along the trail, and the weight would be too much for the wagon.

The children have been complaining this week that I've been coming up with some of the strangest combinations for meals. I told them, "If we can't bring it along to eat later, we're going to eat it now."

All the dried fruit and vegetables we had left from last fall's harvest have been packed in lightweight sacks and hung from the wagon ceilings. The potatoes, carrots, and turnips we have left will be cooked along the way. As it's almost planting season again, we're out of some garden produce. I'll miss the first savory taste of new peas and onions this spring.

I'll take one barrel of pickled cucumbers along to prevent scurvy, but the rest have to find another table to be served from. I was able to trade some of my crocks of pickles and preserves at the general store in Owingsville for staples. But then the decisions of what kind and quality of item to trade for had to be made.

What type of flour, sugar, extra supplies do I really need, and what could I do without? In the past, I've bought fresh ground flour from the gristmill in town when we've needed it, never much ahead. Some people grow their own wheat and haul it in to be ground, but the Pieratts have never bothered growing wheat on our hilly land. The mill keeps so much flour for grinding it and then sells it to customers who don't grow their own wheat crop.

The mill sells different grades of flour. I wish I could have brought superfine flour, sifted several times, to use for delicate cakes and pastry, but it's too expensive and I'm not going to have the time, supplies, or oven to do such baking. I bought the next grade, the middlings, for our cooking. It's much more coarse and granular, but it serves the purpose. Sometimes I've added rye or cornmeal to improve the flavor of this flour.

The mill's shorts, a cross between wheat bran and coarse whole wheat flour, looked clean, so I also bought a 125-pound sack of it. It has to be sifted and you need to add extra liquid when making bread with it, but it can be used as livestock feed in a pinch.

We can't afford to carry the flour in heavy barrels, so it is mostly sacked in fifty-pound quantities in cotton cloth to cut down on weight. Because the flour is not kiln-dried, we double-sacked it in a leather bag. If the flour absorbs too much moisture, I'll end up with a heavy loaf and will have to add more flour to my baking.

Sorghum molasses, our main sweetener, will make the trip in small wooden kegs. We had a big patch of sorghum we harvested and cooked up last fall, so I'm bringing what is left from that batch.

For special occasions, I bought three cones of white sugar. The New Orleans sugar we buy reasonably in the stores here may go for top dollar on the frontier. The cones resemble pointed hats. They are molded at the factory, and wrapped in blue paper. Usually I leave the cones whole and use sugar nippers, a cross between scissors and pliers, to break off lumps as I need them. To save space on the trip, I ground up the cones and divided the two types of sugar (the white sugar on the top gradually changes to brown sugar on the bottom), then sifted it to remove the impurities. The storekeeper said I should pack it in India rubber sacks to keep it dry, but I decided not to add that extra expense. I tucked the cone papers in the wagon because I can extract indigo dye from it to color yarn and material blue.

I also bought a small quantity of low grade brown sugar since it is ten cents cheaper than the cones. It's dark, smelly, sticky, and sometimes dirty, but it still gives sweet taste to cooking.

Parched corn is another sacked commodity in the wagon. The kernels were sun-dried last fall and I'll grind them into cornmeal with the mortar as I need it.

Smoked bacon was double-wrapped in cloth, put in wooden boxes, and covered with bran to prevent the fat from melting during the trip. I cooked the crocks of cut meat I had left into a thick jelly. After it set up in pans and dried, we broke it up into pieces and packed it in tins. If I add boiling water to some pieces, we'll have a portable soup on the trail.

Smaller sacks of beans, rice, salt, saleratus, and coffee are wedged around the whiskey jugs underneath the wagon seat. The medicine box, filled with tiny cloth sachets holding dried medicinal herbs and little medicine bottles, is wedged on top, ready for an emergency.

I put the sacks of yeast cakes, dried bread, and hardtack inside one of the long boxes, along with the box of homemade soap bars. I'll have small sacks of each staple in the back box and refill them from the bigger sacks when I need to.

The back end of the wagon drops down partway on chains and will serve as a preparation table for food or for other jobs. The provision box faces the back so it can be opened up and used without hauling the box out of the wagon every time. It has my tinware, cooking utensils and small sacks of necessities for cooking every day.

I've got tin plates, cups, and silverware enough for the nine of us, plus three extra settings, in case we have company or lose some along the way. I'll have to be careful to count silverware after each meal so the children don't forget and leave it on the ground where they sat for their meal.

Wish I could have brought all my kitchen utensils, but I settled for two spider skillets, three Dutch ovens of various sizes, the reflector for baking, the coffee pot, the coffee mill, the mortar and pestle, a few baking pans, knifes, and my rolling pin.

Walking out to the wagons for the umpteenth time, it struck me that they are starting to look like a peddler's caravan. They are overflowing with items attached to the sides. The wooden washtubs and zinc washboard are fastened to one side of the wagon. The walking plow is lashed on the other side. Small kegs of water, vinegar, and molasses fit in where needed to balance the wagon. Everybody can see what we own because it's hanging in plain sight.

The second wagon is packed even tighter than the first with household and farming tools we'll need after we get to our new land. All the boxes are packed tight so they won't slide around, rattle, or spill. I hope we won't have to unpack it until we get to our destination.

In one of the long storage boxes I packed clothing and extras. Only bare necessities for our family was included. I pressed our good clothes—John's suit, white linen shirts and dark wool trousers for the boys, linsey-woolsey dresses for the girls, Ann, and myself—and carefully packed them in heavy linen sacks. I bet that by next fall some of the clothes will be worn by the next child in line instead of the older brother or sister who used to wear them. New cloth and yarn I spun last fall, along with the spinning wheel, bobbins, and carders are packed. These items will help me make new clothes this fall. I know they will be needed.

I had to leave space to pack in the winter clothes we'll wear on the first leg of the trip until the weather warms up. In the first part of trip we'll be wearing coats and shoes; on the second half we'll be barefoot and shedding our petticoats. The same clothes will be worn all week or so until we stop longer than overnight to wash and dry them. Here at home we never work on Sunday, our day of rest, but I'm afraid that will be the day we get the chance to catch up on chores on the trail.

Another sack holds our family Bible, the few books we own, three writing slates, and pencils that will be used for schooling next fall. I hope there will be other children in the area so we can start a school.

Woodworking tools that aren't needed on the trip were laid in the tool box. The axe and shovel will be kept in the other wagon, within easy reach. I suggested John keep the awl and some bits of buckskin for bridle or saddle repair handy, also. Grain sacks of corn and oats will be used as seed when we plant our new fields. If need be, it could be used for food for us and the animals. Little packets of garden seed, dormant roots of rhubarb and herbs will start my next garden. I even packed peach and apricot stones, and apple seeds in hopes of starting an orchard. At least it gives me comfort that these little seeds will link me to my Kentucky farm.

The bedding we'll use on the trip will be rolled tightly, wrapped with cloth strips, and within easy reach at all times. I hope the girls will be able to take naps during the afternoon as we travel.

The canvas tent I stitched was carefully folded so not to take up much room and was stashed under the wagon seat, within reach.

Being married almost fifteen years, I could have filled one wagon with household furniture alone. Beds, tables, chairs, dressers, the kitchen cupboard. A person just doesn't realize what all she owns until she tries to fit it in a four- by ten-foot wagon. Grandmother's rocker was the only item we included from the furniture in our home. John will have to make beds, a table, and bench seats after we get there.

My sewing basket, cotton and wool batting for quilts, the scrap bag, and the sewing bird clamps I got as an engagement present are tucked in wherever there was a handy gap of space. The folded-down quilting frame was one of the first things put down on the wagon floor, for the boards in it are nine feet long.

My waist pocket, with the essentials of scissors, thimble, thread, needles, and bodkins will keep things I need in hand. (Hidden under my skirt, I will also carry part of our money savings. The other half will be hidden in Ann's pocket.)

Because of our hurriedly planned trip, my sewing was put aside the last six weeks. The Pine Tree quilt blocks I had planned to set with strips and piece together this winter were never finished. I hope to piece blocks together along the way, when I have time.

I've always tried to have a quilt top ready for a spring quilting party. But this spring I have neither the blocks sewn together or my neighbor women to help me quilt it. I wonder who will help me quilt this Pine Tree top together?

A special small satchel was given to me yesterday at the sale by my friends in the neighborhood. Each woman had made a quilt block and embroidered her name on it for me. This fall when I have time to put together this "friendship quilt," I'll remember my friends back in Kentucky.

Ann has quilt tops and quilts of her own along. It's customary to make a baker's dozen of quilt tops for a young woman's dower chest. When the wedding is about to take place, the neighborhood women get together and help finish them. Ann has gone ahead and quilted three of them since she's nearing the spinster age, but she saved her appliqued Rose of Sharon top for her wedding bed, just in case she's proposed to yet.

Many of our mother's things were left to Ann and me. We selected only the items that would be useful to bring along. Many of her linens we gave to nieces for their marriage chests. Her quilt templates, passed down from my grandmother, have to come with us, even if I have to toss out a skillet instead.

Five heavy quilts, stitched by special women in our lives, fill one end of a wooden box. They are packed separate from our bedding. I didn't want these quilts pulled out every day on the trail because they would soon be filled with dust and mud. Some of them have probably never been washed because they are so detailed with fine thread and delicate material.

Father put Mother's all-white Rose of Sharon wedding quilt, with its unusual handmade fringe edging, in my dower chest when it was built. Mother first used the quilt in 1811 and then only for special occasions for thirteen years until she died. It is in perfect condition.

We picked out two other quilts with patterns Ann and I especially like: the Memory Block, made with bits of material from relatives' clothing, and the appliqued Mountain Lily in bright colors. The Slave Chain quilt, stitched by our black mammy, we kept to remind us of the dear woman who took care of us when we were young. I remember her being so superstitious about quilt patterns that she only used ones with wavy lines. She was sure that evil spirits followed the straight lines in quilts.

Wrapped in an old sheet, the aged yellowed quilt of Elizabeth Ayrie Pieratt, John's French grandmother, is placed between other quilts. She gave the quilt to me when we announced our engagement. Elizabeth was no longer able to sew anymore and couldn't help with my quilts, so she gave me one of hers. It was old when I got it, and being young, I didn't appreciate its value at first. It's a huge quilt, over ten feet square when you count the twenty-inch gathered flounce around the edge. Made in the olden days, it is sized for a six- to-seven foot bed built to hold the entire family. The Liberty quilt, which was popular around the Revolution days, has faded blocks of eagles, wreaths of stars, and flags on it. Looking at it again I realize there are only thirteen stars on these flags. Our modern flags now have thirty-one. I remember her saying this quilt was made by her friends when she got married in Baltimore to Valentine. That was almost sixty-five years ago.

And I couldn't part with Levi's baby quilt, with the date of his birth and death stitched in the corner. It was the first quilt I made after we were married. I never used it for another child because he died wrapped in it. Seeing this quilt is the only way I can remember his face.

So many of the items I had planned to take were left behind. I hesitated but I finally packed my dinnerware and a few glass dishes in a barrel of straw. I'm a little worried that the container will be an easy thing to toss out if we need to take off weight. I made sure it wasn't near the back within easy reach. John kept saying, "Pack light or you'll have the misery of seeing it tossed alongside the road if we have to lighten the load," and I know he meant it.

March 15, 1854

It's as if I am walking through a deserted world this morning. Everything is shrouded in the heavy mist that envelops Kentucky in the wee morning hours of spring. Sounds seem to be absent from man, beast, and nature. The thick, damp fog muffles the turning of our wagon wheels as we follow the trail that parallels Slate Creek. The slivers of slate rock that form the bottom and sides of the stream seem extra cold, wet, and dark this morning. The bare branches on the white-barked sycamores that line the water's edge are limp, dripping with moisture, silent, not moving a breath, as if they mourn our leaving, too.

As the swirling mist of gray dawn closed around our log cabin minutes ago, I tried to burn the picture of it in my mind forever. John said someday we'll be back to visit family, but I know I will never see Kentucky again.

I glance at my cold, bundled children trudging along the trail beside the wagons. Their faces buried under woolen hats and scarfs, they watch their step around the ruts in the trail.

Our children have mixed feelings about the trip. My three sons initially thought of this trip as their adventure into manhood. Its seriousness dawned on them this morning and they have been silent, except for an occasional sniffle and the wiping of a nose on a coat sleeve. Little do they know how many miles their feet will tread to their future.

Belvard, at twelve, and eight-year-old Robby never question their father's stern wisdom. They both look like him—light-brown hair, thin chiseled faces with such deep-set eyes you can never tell what they are thinking. James Monroe, my ten-year-old, is another story. With dark hair and stark blue eyes in a round face like mine, he is always questioning the rhyme and reason of everything.

Sarah and George Ann, at five and four, have no idea what lies ahead of them except the reserved gloom they sense from me. Their chubby cheeks are red from the cold, and they're trying to keep up with the rest of us.

Yesterday my mischievous pair was determined to pack their favorite cat somewhere in the wagon boxes. Luckily the cat always managed to give its hiding place away when it got tired of being confined. I haven't found the courage to tell the girls they will never see their grandmas or Kentucky cousins again.

At least it helps that James and Mary's five young boys are along on the trip. Jimmy, age eight, stairstepping down to Albert, Will, Johnny, and Little Valentine, are close playmates to my children.

At the last minute, Nellie Tipton, Mary's sister, decided to travel with us to help with her nephews. Unmarried, and with no matrimonial proposal in sight at age forty-seven, she is more game to experience the frontier than the rest of us women. She threw a small parcel of belongings into the wagon this morning and was raring to go. I hope her stamina can keep up with her enthusiasm.

My baby, Emma, squirms to get down. She wants her freedom to explore her new world, but she'll have to watch from the safety of my arms. The trip will be the hardest on our children.

Emma makes me think of last night when I visited our eldest son's grave. We met at Sarah's to eat supper with all of the family one last time. I slipped away from the gathering before the light of sunset faded away. My son is buried with other generations on the sloping hill behind the Pieratt homestead. Levi was only four months old when he died. He was my firstborn. I'll never forget the anticipation of the first child, the panic of the first delivery, the joy of the first son, the pain of the first loss.

14

We're slowly making our way down the road past the road-house now. For some reason, a clear pocket of sky opens up and the house is visible to us. Sarah stands outside the door, trying to catch a glimpse of us as we go by. She doesn't wave. I don't know if she can't see us on the road down below her or if she chooses not to say good-bye. Her forlorn figure will be my last memory of Sarah.

Going past my birthplace brings a flood of tears that stream down my face. The memories of growing up with my brothers, my father's laughter, my faded three-year-old image of my mother and the love of my stepmother hit me all at once. This place has always been my refuge when times were hard during my adult life. Betsy was the first person I told about our move.

Suddenly, as if called up by my mind, she appears walking by my side. Betsy had been waiting for us at the end of her lane for one last good-bye. She hands me a chest that I recognize as my father's writing box. Inside are sheets of paper, two quill pens, a bottle of ink, my father's wax seal, and a bag of coins for mailing letters.

"Please write," is all she says before she gives me a tight hug and steps out of the way.

Then the fog seals behind me, never to let me enter my past again.

Hot Wax and Tears

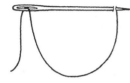

Wednesday evening, March 15, 1854
by Hinkston Creek in Kentucky

Dear Betsy,

After three hours on the trail, the men decided to stop for nooning, our midday break. Both the animals and children (and their mothers) were ready for the stop.

The teams aren't used to traveling together and caused some problems this morning. The oxen gratefully let Belvard and John take their yokes off, and they meandered to join the herd. I thought it would take a while to get the animals to stop and quiet down, but they dropped their heads immediately to graze. The milk cow's rope was staked by the herd to keep her from wandering again. John had tied the cow to the back of the provisions wagon this morning after he had to go back twice to get her. The poor cow kept trying to run back to her barn. John, on horseback, was able to catch her after Robby yelled that she had turned tail. In a few weeks she'll be about ready to calf and doesn't like the idea of doing it away from the familiar spot where she had her last calves. After the calf is born, she'll quiet down.

Blackie, our dog, is slightly confused, especially when John turned back towards home. He didn't know whether to stay with me and the wagons or chase after John and the cow. I hope he sticks around tonight and doesn't try to follow our trail back to the farm. We need Blackie along for protection.

I didn't bother starting a fire to cook our nooning meal. Yesterday I cooked a ham and two chickens, baked bread and pies that I hope will last us a few meals. Before we left, I filled up my kettles and pans with food. When they're empty, I'll have to start cooking on the trail. I still had to unpack the tinware to serve it on, though.

Balancing our plates of food on our knees, we perched lopsided on the wagon tongues so as not to sit on the wet ground. It will be a long time before we all sit together at a table again. The children were tired enough on our first day to eat without whining about a cold meal. Sarah and George Ann grew drowsy on their perch when the sun finally showed its face and warmed their backs. I climbed into the front of the wagon and laid out a bedroll so the girls could take a nap.

Emma and Valentine were so happy to finally be free from our arms that they toddled around to explore everything in their sight. After Emma wore herself out, I nursed her, then squeezed her between the two older girls in the bed. Thankfully, their naps in the wagon lasted partway into our afternoon trek.

We're camped in the bottom of a valley on Hinkston Creek, east of Mount Sterling, tonight. We only went ten miles today. We had hoped for more than that, but it will take time to get through these hills and for us all to adjust to life on the trail.

Between the walking and the pale sun, we finally warmed up by midafternoon, but it turned bone-chilling when the sun sank below the hills this evening. It started out as a gray, gloomy day and it ended the same way. Sadness still echoes in my empty heart for the family we left behind.

This first letter is sealed with hot wax and tears,

Deborah

Thursday evening, March 16, 1854
north of Mt. Sterling on Stoner Creek

Dear Betsy,

This morning I couldn't figure out why there was a rooster crowing directly in my ear. I thought I was dreaming until he did it again and I realized my head was just inches away from the chickens' cage that's hooked to the back of the wagon. It took a few seconds after I opened my eyes and stared at the inside circle of the wagon top to realize where I was. I was cold, stiff from the boards and boxes I slept on, and I missed John's warmth. Until the weather warms up, Ann, the girls, and I are sleeping in the furnishings wagon. John and the boys are in the provisions wagon. Eventually we will sleep on the ground under the tent we brought along, but it's too cold and muddy to do that yet as far as I'm concerned. I'd rather keep the children in the wagons to keep them safe anyway.

Trying not to disturb the girls, who miraculously slept through our morning reveille, I opened the hole in the wagon canvas and slipped out onto the seat to put on my shoes. I didn't bother taking any clothes off last night since I was so cold. In the early dawn light I saw shadows moving around the wagons as the adults tended to private matters and got ready to start the day.

The campfire still had a few warm embers in it that flared alive when I added more sticks. Last night I drew water from the creek to let the sediment settle in the pail. Skimming off the top water this morning made a fairly clear pot of water for the coffee. I roasted the green coffee beans in a skillet, then ground them in the grinder before adding them to the boiling water.

John milked the cow first thing this morning and poured some in each cup for the children, a bowl of it for the dog, and put the rest in a tin bucket for noon. I sliced bread and buttered it for our breakfast, then woke our brood.

We made much better time today. Hills were rolling, but not rough and rocky. John told the boys that the trail we're following has been here for centuries. There are numerous salt licks in Kentucky, so dozens of well-worn woods buffalo trails connect them together. Buffalo always selected the easiest route, easiest grade, and most direct course. Since they needed water, their paths always intersected creeks and rivers at the easiest crossing points. Over time these paths were used by the Indians and then widened as the white settlers moved in and formed towns along these routes.

The exposed cliffs along this part of the trail have a distinct green tint to them. Robby is fascinated with rocks and wanted to collect specimens along the trip. John sternly told him we can't add extra weight to the wagon for the oxen to pull, or else Robby would be trying to pick up rocks bigger than himself to add to his collection.

As tight as I thought we packed the boxes in the wagon, we had to repack some before we started out this morning. Yesterday afternoon something sounded like it was loose, and it slid up and down with the hills and thumped when the wagon wheels hit bad spots on the road. After much digging around, we figured it was the hammer inside the tool box.

Finally getting some good progress, with fourteen miles covered today. The animals are getting used to the trail, and we moved along better. The weather was cool and crisp, not bleak and damp like yesterday.

When we were at the top of the first ascent this morning we looked back to where we started yesterday. Rising above the morning mist, the ridges of Bath County were in the distance. I stopped and stared for a moment. That was the last time I'll see those hills again.

It made me wonder what you did today. Probably went about your normal routine. As you prepare for bedtime, too, are you thinking about us at this moment and wondering how far we've gone?

Wishing the distance between us wasn't expanding each day,

Deborah

Sunday afternoon, March 19, 1854
west of Lexington on South Elkhorn Creek

Dear Betsy,

Extra heavy dew on the grass yesterday morning wet my skirt and petticoats halfway up my knees and kept me chilled and cross most of the day. It was one of those days when nothing seemed to go right. John rightfully remarked about the burned breakfast this morning, the children bickered about the most trivial things, and the dog ate the eggs out of the basket that Robby forgot to set inside the wagon.

Things seemed to progress from bad to worse by late evening when we couldn't find water to camp by. We must always look for a good place to camp for the livestock, not the family. The oxen need water and grass to keep up their strength. We ended up traveling fifteen miles to the South Elkhorn Creek before calling it a night.

We could have camped outside of Lexington, but the men thought we could go a few more miles after we got there. John was grumbling about paying tolls to use the pikes going through Lexington, so I think he wasn't in the mood to stop and see this fine city. We went this way originally so we wouldn't have to pay the tolls along the Iron Works Pike that runs from Owingsville to Frankfort, but we found a pole across this road, too.

I would have loved to look around town today when we had "spare" time. The road goes right through town, so we got a glimpse of it. The tower of a church loomed to the north of Main Street and I heard the Transylvania University is up there too. Large brick homes showed prominent, rich people live here. I remember that Senator Henry Clay was from Lexington.

We walked past the Fayette County Courthouse and there was a slave auction going on to the west of the building. I felt so bad for the black woman standing there weeping as her children were being sold off and separated. I don't see how slaveholders can split them up, but that is a way of life around here.

When we finally stopped last night, I didn't bother starting a fire. We were so exhausted, I just gave everyone a handful of hardtack, which we ate while crawling into bed.

21

The children were exhausted and slept well last night. Our muscles reacted to yesterday's jaunt up and down the hills that were more rugged and rocky than any we have crossed so far. The girls wanted to ride on the wagon seat, but I made them walk instead. I'm afraid the rough jarring will knock them off the seat and throw them in the path of the wagon wheels.

They have been real troupers the first days on the road, but it may be wearing thin. George Ann asked this morning if we could go back home now because she misses her Grandmas. I miss our family, too.

We're staying by this creek and resting today. Or I should say some of us are. The men have spent part of the day catching up on their sleep. John and James have been taking turns staying awake at night to watch over the wagons and herd, so they took advantage of our quiet day.

The boys are lying around keeping an eye on the animals as they graze the lush new growth around the creek. We'll try to stop on Sundays to give the animals a rest. If the oxen play out, we can't go on.

We've finally gotten a break in the weather. Strong sunlight came out for the first time on our journey, and I finally felt that I got the chill out of my bones. Of course it helped that I was up to my elbows in hot water to wash a few clothes that had gotten very muddy. I was working up a sweat by the time I hauled water from the creek up to heat in the big kettle over our campfire. Couldn't get things real clean in creek water, but at least got the mud-caked socks and petticoats to look a little better. The hard part is getting things to dry. We hung a rope from the outside of the wagon to a tree to hang clothes on. Tonight we'll move the line and clothes inside the wagon so they won't get wet again overnight from the dew.

Ann made the first attempt to bake bread since we left. She put the dough in the Dutch oven to rise by the fire first. When the dough had risen to the right height, Ann put it in the fire and heaped ashes on top of the lid to bake the bread evenly. We didn't know how long to bake it over an open fire instead of in our kitchen's hearth. Ann couldn't check it without peeking under the lid and having ashes blow in on top of the dough. When Ann finally pulled it out of the Dutch oven and sliced it, there were a few ashes mixed in the crust, so she peeled off the top layer and gave it to the chickens.

Had time to boil beans today, then put them to bake for supper. Added a slice of ham for flavor. When I baked beans at home, I didn't realize how many hours it took. We just put the beans in the fireplace and went about other business for the rest of the day. Now we're usually not in one place long enough to keep a fire going for several hours.

Soaked dried pumpkin slices for a pie. I had to wait until the chickens laid some eggs before I could stir up the filling. Rolling out the crust was a little frustrating because the wagon end we use for a table is much higher than the table in my kitchen. I couldn't get the leverage I needed until I stood on an overturned pail. Turned out pretty well baked in the reflector. With limited baking utensils along, I have to plan the meal around what I can fit in the skillet, or the kettles.

We figured out the best way to lay the fire is dig a twelve-inch trench, about three foot long, and lay the kindling in it. There is less chance of the fire blowing out and starting a wildfire, and we can set pans directly over the fire, using the edges of the pit for support.

Did I tell you we found an easy way to churn butter this week? On our second day out, I hung the tin pail with the cream in the wagon and at noon I had clumps of butter swimming in buttermilk! The constant motion of the swinging bucket churned the butter. It doesn't make a solid lump, but it's enough for fresh butter every day.

Missing a quiet, restful Sunday at "home,"

Deborah

Monday evening, March 20, 1854
east bank of the Kentucky River

Dear Betsy,

We're finally getting into a more open, flat area. The soil is better here than anywhere we've seen so far in Kentucky. Farms seem to be bigger and better looking, too.

Today we went by the largest house I've ever seen. It was what would be considered a plantation house, not a rough log home, but one with white-painted boarding on the sides and porch pillars on front. John said the owner probably came from the Deep South. I've never seen a place so big. Course, I've never been this far from home, either, to see such sights. Dingy, small slave cabins contrasted sharply to the owner's house. Four large tobacco barns, with their long boards spaced for aeration, showed the landlord owned many acres. We followed the farm's split-rail fence for a mile and so had time to eye the place.

It's a balmy spring day today, and little children both black and white were playing together in the sunshine beside the big house. Young colts frolicked beside their mothers in the pasture by a well-built barn. Barefoot slaves, men and women, were working the warmed red soil to prepare the tobacco seed beds. John says they grow hemp, cotton, and sheep for wool in this area of the state.

It seems unusual to people watching our wagons go by that we don't have slaves with us. Kentucky isn't a big slave state, but most families we've seen along the way have one or two slaves for help around the farm.

John strongly opposes the use of black people as animals to do our work, and I think that was one of the deciding factors in our move. Kansas will become a free state and we won't have to worry what people think about our way of life. Remember when my father gave John four slaves as my dowry when we got married in '39? John set them free immediately by giving them freedom papers and a passage across the Ohio River. He could have sold them for a thousand dollars each to a big plantation holder down in Mississippi, but he saw through the color of their skin and knew they were people just like us. It seemed unusual to me at the time, since I grew up with the slaves and they were part of our family. But given the choice, I was happy to see them set out on their own journey to the North. I've always wondered what happened to them. Since that time I've seen the slave situation in a different light. I hope the slaves we see today are treated well.

The eleven miles we traveled today slowly descended down a winding trail that led to the banks of the Kentucky River. It's the largest stream I've ever seen. Many other wagons are camped here on the east bank to take their turn at crossing the river. It's wide and deep enough that we'll have to pay to have the wagons ferried across tomorrow.

After we took care of the animals, we had a little time to look around before we needed to start the evening meal. The riverbank shoots straight up to the northeast of where we're camped. Some other campers had climbed up and down the hill, so we decided to do some exploring, too. When we got to the top of the hill, you could see for miles! Fresh green grass cropping up along the riverbanks made it look a ribbon edged in bright emerald green. The grass hasn't turned blue yet since it isn't blooming time. From this point we could see the river wind its way south until the landscape colors faded into the horizon.

Right on the very edge of the bluff was a cemetery overlooking the river. We walked around the graves, reading the names of the departed. As the girls picked early lavender violets that blanketed the ground around the grave of Daniel Boone and his wife, Rebecca, I told them about the burial that took place here in '45, when they moved his body from a Missouri cemetery. How they had a long procession behind the hearse pulled by four white horses, and a service at the grave site with a huge gathering of people. I remember that the whole state knew about.

I know this legend died before I was born, but I've heard stories about how he blazed trails into Kentucky and farther west. Now we're traveling along the very trail he first cut through to Missouri.

The graves on the bluff made me feel melancholy tonight. It made me realize we won't be buried by our families in Kentucky. Why didn't I think of that before now? I suppose my mind was occupied with the move and I blocked that thought until now. Maybe, like Daniel Boone, who actually died elsewhere, I'll come back to rest in Kentucky, as he did. One never knows what the future has in store, in this life or the next.

Wishing you were here to see the trailblazers,

Deborah

Tuesday evening, March 21, 1854
Frankfort, Kentucky

Dear Betsy,

This morning was such a contrast to other quiet mornings by a small creek by ourselves. Probably forty to fifty wagons and carts spent the night around us. Late into the night we could hear a variety of noise from the different groups. One wagonload of people was singing hymns, while at the next tent rowdy talking and card playing was going on. Curiosity stole sleep from my boys last night. I caught them peeking out the back of the wagon, staring at the wonderment of it all. John was at another campfire talking to some travelers and didn't notice his charges.

But people were up in the early hours before dawn, starting their fires for breakfast like they had gotten a good night's sleep. Herders were rounding up the animals, milking the cows, saddling the horses, and yoking the oxen up to the wagons. Breakfast was over by six-thirty, tents packed and wagons loaded. Then everyone got in line to cross the river and waited their turn.

By noon we still had several wagons in front of us to cross. We munched on cold meat and bread while we waited to move forward. It was fascinating to see how the wagons were loaded on to the ferry, centered to distribute the weight, and then lashed down to keep it there. By the time I was trying to coax our oxen onto the floating ferry, I wasn't so sure I wanted my family on the raft, let alone our oxen. It pitched and rolled a little as I stood with my hand on the lead oxen's nose to keep him calm. I could just picture the wagon sliding off the edge of the planks with all six children inside. But there was no other way to get across. The little creeks we crossed so far were nothing more than draws with a little water in them. This was something else.

By the time we got our four wagons across, I was a wreck. And then John reminds me we have several more rivers to cross that make this one look like a large creek! John and James had to swim the herd across the river. I was worried for them and our milk cow, but all made it across safely this time. Dry clothes had to be unpacked for John after the wet crossing. I hope he doesn't catch his death of cold.

We camped on the other side of the river after the crossing and decided to explore the town. We left the wagons and children in Nellie and Ann's charge and followed the riverfront street with James and Mary. We had seen many travelers using India rubber items, and James wanted to check the prices before we left a trading area. And I had an apron pocket full of letters that I wanted to mail to you while we were near a town, too.

Frankfort, Kentucky's capital city, is cuddled in the bend on the west side of the Kentucky River. People bustled up and down the streets doing their shopping. It was a mixture of poor home-spun travelers like us needing travel supplies, and city folks with tailored clothes, hats, and parasols doing their daily shopping. I felt out of place and shabby, but Mary reminded me that these people would never see me again, so what was the difference? Thank goodness I rubbed my dress hem with a stiff clothes brush to get the cakes of dried mud off before we came into town, or people would really have had their noses out of joint.

I could have spent a day just gawking in the store windows. There are so many more stores here, with a wider variety of things, compared to Owingsville.

The milliner's window, with its fancy hats of ribbons and trimmings made me chuckle out loud. Can you imagine me on this journey, trudging every dirty mile, wearing a hat with fabric flowers and a bird stuck on the rim? I'd be the laughingstock at every river crossing.

One general store specialized in outfitting travelers. It had everything from barrels of crackers and salt pork to wagon parts and oxen yokes.

I was amazed at all the India rubber items you could buy—coats, leggings, sacks of all sizes. India rubber tarps that could be used to cover boxes or laid on the ground under your bedroll to keep you dry. The storekeeper explained that melted India rubber is pushed into a fabric, then dusted with sulphur to set the rubber. Remembering how long we stayed wet one drizzly day, I eyed the treated material, thinking about making clothing with it, but decided we could do without this expense. It would be nice if everyone in our family could have a waterproof garment. John has a good gutta-percha poncho, which keeps him dry most of the time. I make do with my shawls, and the children can climb in the wagon when it's raining hard. Besides, I don't have the time to make clothes anyway.

Ann had a good supper going when we got back to the wagons. The smells of fresh-brewed coffee and stewed apples drifted to our nostrils before we set foot in our little camp. The stop here in Frankfort has done her good. Ann's delicate health has withstood the trip so far, but I worry that all the hills we've climbed the past few days has about worn her out. We all had hoped her health would improve on the trip. I had a little money left over in my pocket after mailing your letters, so I bought a little chocolate powder to make Ann a cup of hot chocolate for her cough. She said thank you (you too, since it was bought with your money) and tucked it away for when she feels like she needs the special hot drink. Don't worry about Ann. I'm sure we'll see an improvement in her health as the weather and roads get better.

Thank you for your generous gifts to us, now and in the past,

Deborah and Ann

Sunday afternoon, March 26, 1854
Louisville, Kentucky

Dear Betsy,

Since I last wrote, we've camped on the Guist Creek, then on a farm by the Plum Creek. All these small creeks we've crossed lately have had plenty of clear water to drink, but not enough to hamper our crossing. This man whose farm we stopped at had been to Frankfort for supplies and happened to strike up a conversation with James at a store. He invited us to travel with him until we got to his place. John bought a little corn from the man to supplement our oxens' grazing. My mouth watered when the wife offered me a fresh loaf of white bread straight out of the oven. I offered to pay or exchange something for it, but she insisted I take it, saying she knows it will be a long time before we get oven-fresh bread again. Someday I'll repay her generosity by helping another traveling woman who stops by my door.

Friday night we stopped at the edge of Jeffersontown. We definitely haven't felt like lone travelers on this stretch, since this is the main road between Frankfort and Louisville. Strangers have traveled with us the whole way. I sold fried quick bread and stew every night to an old grizzled man who welcomed the chance to eat with us instead of lighting a fire and cooking for himself. I put the money he paid me in my stocking for safekeeping until I could transfer it to my hiding place.

Saturday we drove through the streets of Louisville and pulled into the crowded campground on the Ohio River's edge. It looks like we'll spend another night or two here waiting to cross.

John was right. At a mile wide, the Ohio River is much bigger than the last river. I wonder how many more rivers we'll have to cross by ferry. Thinking of the alternative of having to cross them without help, has eased my mind, though. Before the ferry was built, people had to make their own rafts, unpack their wagons, and move the possessions over a few at a time with numerous trips. I guess I've talked myself into being thankful for those rolling rafts that scare me to death. We'll have plenty of opportunity to see the ferry in action because there are more wagons here to cross than there was at the Kentucky River ferry. We hope we can cross tomorrow.

We walked upstream to see the Falls of the Ohio. It is a cascade of rapids that flow over a section of rock riverbed. It drops twenty-six feet over a two-and-a-half-mile stretch. Because it's spring, it was a froth of white sprays billowing down the river. In summer—when the water level is down—this is the only place along the whole length of the Ohio River where a person can walk across the river. Bison used it during their migration, then the Indians. Traders found the area and eventually settlements developed. We also saw the canal that was built in the river channel in the 1820s to allow boats to cross this shallow section of river.

To put your mind at ease, I should tell you that the children have adjusted well to the trail. All eleven have arrived thus far without a sniffle or major scratch. They walk ahead of the slow oxen, but always in sight, or else one of us yells for them. The younger ones pick up treasures—rocks, flowers, insects, and try to stick them in the wagon. Little apron and pant pockets can hold a surprise at bedtime. The nooning time finds them playing games or exploring the area after their meal and chores. Afternoons usually find the little ones sleeping in the wagons while they roll along the trail.

The oxen seem to be well broken in to the trail. Whoever is driving the teams needs to crack the whip occasionally when the oxen have to pull hard, but they usually respond well to voice commands. Belvard has command over the first wagon, James Monroe the second. Mary's oldest, Jimmy, has their first wagon, and Nellie or my Robby help with their second one. The men are still riding horseback most of the time behind the herd, but they occasionally get off and walk for a while in the afternoon when the animals are plodding along at a slower pace.

I've caught up on washing today. The yellow-orange soil common in this part of Kentucky has coated our wagon and clothes with its tint. The washcloth I used to clean Emma's face after dinner had an orange hue to it after I was done.

Her diapers will be permanently orange with a few more washings in creek water, but at least they are halfway clean and better-smelling. The first wet days on the road, all I could do was scrape the soiled diapers, dry them over the fire, and refold them a different direction. I found out I couldn't get them dry enough by entirely washing them out. I was afraid the poor child would get a bad case of diaper rash, but her little bottom survived with a little cornstarch dusting until that first Sunday's wash.

We've met some interesting people who are waiting for their turn at crossing, too. Most are from Kentucky, but one family is from Pennsylvania. The wife's dress isn't much different from mine, but as soon as I heard her talk, I knew she was from the North. Another clue was that she milked the cow instead of her husband doing the job, like the men do in the South.

I couldn't figure what she was doing with her last night's milk, so I asked out of curiosity. She dipped the thick cream into a clean cloth bag, then hung it up to let the liquid drip out. When the liquid was gone, she mixed in just a little salt and had a soft spread to put on bread. It's called a Dutch cheese. She didn't add any rennet or heat, so it was a perfect way to use up cream on the trail. She gave me enough to serve on bread tonight, so I shared some of our extra eggs I had stashed in the flour sack. She didn't have any chickens along, so she was thrilled for the exchange.

Comparing quilt patterns also showed we were from different states. I traced her a Sassafras Leaf and she gave me the Dutchman's Puzzle. Some patterns we compared are the same or very similar, but have different names. I have enclosed the pattern for your collection, too.

We've adapted to outdoor cooking as long as the weather cooperates. Ann's baking treat this long stop was molasses gingerbread. The smell of that drifting around the campfire made more than just our young boys' mouth water. I think Ann could pick up a husband along the way if she keeps treating all the bachelors to her good cooking.

Adapting to the trail,

Deborah

32

Pickles Downstream

Monday evening, March 27, 1854
camped in Indiana

Dear Betsy,

I don't know if I feel doomed or resolved as I write this letter. I do know I could spill out a gallon of tears right now if I was alone. I was starting to feel like I was adapting to the situation and getting along fine on the trail. Now the fears and panic that I felt when the decision was first made are creeping back into my mind.

After waiting two days, we're safely across the Ohio River and into the state of Indiana. We're camped on the knobs west of New Albany tonight. From here we can see New Albany and Louisville. Even though we're just a few miles from Kentucky, it feels different to me. It's probably the regrettable feeling that we are out of Kentucky. Before we crossed the wide Ohio River, I felt in my heart that we could still turn around and go back home, simply because we were still in Kentucky.

Yesterday, when we looked to the west, this hill we're camped on now had a bright smoky halo around it. I remember thinking that it looked like a silver lining, a good omen. Up close it's a dreary gray cloud of gloom instead.

Another thing that has pulled down my optimism is that we witnessed an accident at the river yesterday. It really hit home because it happened to the Pennsylvania family who camped by us as we both waited to cross the river.

We crossed early this morning, just before them, and were still near the bank's edge to see what happened. When the ferry hauling their wagon was halfway across the river, it tilted. I heard screams and bellows, looked up, and saw the wagon slide off the edge. I don't know if the wagon was overloaded, the weight was unevenly distributed, or just the wind and water pushed it over. The woman, holding the oxen, was thrown to the floor on the ferry, but her children were inside the wagon bed. Jumping off and swimming to the wagon, she tried desperately to reach them, but the wagon top prevented them from getting out. It only took seconds for the water to rush into the wagon and sink it. Her husband had been with their animals, so he wasn't on the ferry with them. They lost their family, the wagon with the oxen yoked to it, and all their belongings in a blink of the eye. I don't know if the couple will go on or turn back to Pennsylvania. I just can't imagine losing all my children like that at once. This will haunt me the rest of the trip and make me fearful of river crossings from now on. I'll never leave Emma in the wagon for a ferry ride again, that's for sure!

Gloomy weather has returned to add to our misery. Drizzle, fog, and slippery roads were our companions today as we crossed the rugged range of hills that run north and south through this area. Since it didn't turn to hard rain, we kept trudging along, but only got a few miles. Before we stopped for nooning, tiny sharp sleet was slicing at our faces. The little ones did not challenge our order to ride in the wagons today.

Although we tried for over an hour, we couldn't keep a fire going. I leaned over it with a skillet to shield the fire pit while Ann lit matches to kindling. All we got was smoke in our eyes until the next rainy gust blew out our latest attempt. We finally gave up and settled for hardtack, leftover beans, and dried jerky.

Downcast like the weather,

Deborah

Wednesday evening, March 29, 1854
west side of the Blue River

Dear Betsy,

The last two days has been soggy traveling up and down more knobs. Went through Greenville yesterday. The soil is red and sandy here, with poor quality wild grass growing in some areas; it is thickly matted with brush in others. Shrubs along the water's edge here have swollen buds, not much further along than the bushes we left in Kentucky two weeks ago. Accidently found some sink holes than caused problems with a wagon.

Today we traveled on a high ridge that overlooked a wooded area that lies to the south of the trail. With a little imagination, from one high point I could imagine that the trees would be a beautiful sight of orange-red and yellow-gold in the fall sunshine. I'd like to see the trees in the spring sunshine, too, but we don't seem to be that lucky this week.

We forged the Blue River today. It was slightly up because of the light rain, but we could cross it with caution. John waded across first on horseback to see how deep it was. It looked like the water might be high enough to seep in the wagon beds, so the boys caulked the cracks between the boards with pitch from the tar bucket that always hangs from the back of the wagon.

The main problem was getting the team and wagon down and back up the slippery sides. We cut and piled brush on the banks to help with the footing for the animals and added the extra team of oxen to help pull the wagons up the banks. There was a great deal of yelling and swearing by the men by the time the crossing was over.

I'm afraid our bad luck of witnessing wagon accidents continues, although there were no fatalities this time except for food.

After we got across, another group crossed at the same point, except one wagon shifted downstream a little before the team attempted to come up. Apparently a wheel hit a large rock underneath the water's surface that we had all missed. The jolt broke the rear axle, the right back wheel popped off, the wagon leaned over, and the end gate flopped open. The woman's pickle barrel bounced out, broke open, and then there were pickles floating downstream.

We all splashed in to help carry their belongings to the dry shore before they got any wetter. If we would have had time, and an empty wagon, we could have driven up to the broken wagon and exchanged the load.

When the wagon was empty, the teams were able to drag it out of the river. The owner had some spare wagon parts, but he may have to go back to Greenville if he doesn't have the right ones. It was getting very dark when they finally got the wagon out, so repairs will have to wait until tomorrow. Someone said we're a few days away from the trading post at French Lick, so they'll travel on to restock their provisions there instead of having to cross this river to get back to Greenville again.

Sacks of flour and cornmeal were ruined, sugar dissolved, and clean white shirts the woman had packed turned a dirty river brown. We spread the soaked beans and dried fruit out to dry on their tent, but they really need several warm sunny days to do any good. We exchanged some of her wet beans for our dry beans to help out. Her beans are cooking up in all our pots tonight and she got a partial sack of dry beans from us to cook with for the next few days. This episode made me think of those India rubber sacks we saw in Frankfort. Wouldn't they have been a blessing to this woman today?

Thanking our lucky stars we missed that rock,

Deborah and John

Friday evening, March 31, 1854
French Lick, Indiana

Dear Betsy,

We crossed the Patoka Creek without incident, but the weather has just gotten too bad to travel. We've stopped by French Lick until the road is passable again. The heavy wheels were getting stuck in mud and it was too hard on the oxen to try to keep pulling up and down the hills.

This wooded settlement is the halfway point between Louisville and Vincennes, following the Buffalo Trace Trail we're on. The trading post and hotels were busy places with this weather.

Travelers with us bet we could smell the town before we could see it, and they were right. There are several sulphur springs in the area that give off a distinct smell of rotten eggs.

We bought grain for the animals since the grass is still thin and the oxen have worked so hard this week. We camped on the west side of town, a little downwind from the springs we parked by. The animals are attracted to the springs and love to lick the minerals off the rocks around the water hole.

The clerk at the trading post said the water won't hurt us or the animals, so we let them drink out of the springs. He did warn us that drinking too much of the water would have a laxative effect, though. The children don't like the taste of the sulphured water, so I added vinegar and sugar for a drink. We figured out that pouring the water through cornmeal absorbs some of the sulphur taste.

For a while yesterday the heavens opened up and it just poured. We climbed into the wagons and tried to keep occupied by reciting poems and doing hand games. This is the most time I've had to work on my quilt blocks since we left home. Mary's wagon rocked with the boys singing tunes to James's fiddle playing. Nellie can outsing them all, and I could tell she was setting the pace.

The kindling in our fire pit was floating in water instead of burning by the time the storm quit. Ann forgot about the bread dough she had sitting on the end gate. It was a thin, soupy batter when she finally remembered it.

Lunch was hardtack and remembering all the work it took to make it. Every other night for two weeks we mixed a batch and I made the whole family take turns kneading, rolling, and cutting it into squares. It had to dry rock-hard before we packed it in bags, then wooden boxes. We're all tired of eating it, but it sure beats hunger when you can't keep a campfire going.

Wishing for hot tea and dry clothes,

Deborah

Sunday evening, April 2, 1854
east fork of the White River

Dear Betsy,

Since we lost time on the trail due to rain and slippery roads, we traveled today. It may be Sunday by the calendar, it doesn't really matter when you're trying to get somewhere. After spending two days in camp, everyone, animals included, seemed to be ready to leave this morning. We traveled about thirteen miles to the east fork of the White River. Ever since we crossed the Blue River, we've been traveling under a thick canopy of trees. This area of rich bottomland is heavy timbered with oak, hickory, walnut, cherry, and other trees we couldn't identify.

Today we passed out of the wooded area and a beautiful view of the plains lay before us. The sea of grass seemed to wave on forever to the west.

We followed the White River upstream a ways until it narrowed enough that we would cross without problems. This tributary starts at the top of a bluff, so we did not go any farther than we had to.

The rains have stopped but the air is still cold. Feels like winter weather is back. Coats are a necessity again. Ann eyed her powdered chocolate tonight, but instead of using it, she deeply inhaled its fragrance and put the lid back on the tin.

It's been hard to start the campfire this week with only wet wood available. John has taken the axe and stripped the inner bark off of trees to have something dry for kindling. I've tried to keep the jar that holds the friction matches shut tight at all times because they will not strike when damp. I can tell moisture is starting to seep in there, too.

This afternoon we chanced upon a small flock of ducks as we trailed the river. John was fortunate enough to bag one for our supper tonight. It is roasting in the reflector oven with wild onions as I write to you. I saved the plucked feathers and put them in an empty cloth sack for a pillow.

Belvard cleaned the guns tonight, dried them carefully, and then oiled them. Wet weather makes guns rusty and unsafe, and we can't afford an accident on this trip.

Ann noticed when she made stick bread tonight that the flour is getting damp. When we get into sunny warm weather, we need to open up the sacks to dry the flour out.

Did I tell you about our quick and easy way to make bread? We have one special flour sack, and we pour water in the middle of it, then poke a branch into the middle of the flour mass. Stick the branch with the glob of dough on it in the ground by the fire, turn it a few times, and you have a quick bread you don't have to use a pan for. First time we saw someone do that, we wondered "what in the world?" But now we do it, too.

Finding new ways to enjoy our bread on the trail,

Deborah

Monday evening, April 3, 1854
farmer's yard

Dear Betsy,

All the farms in Indiana that we've passed by have been well kept. This area has been farmed for about three or four decades, so homesteads, orchards, and towns are well established.

We haven't seen any field work done yet since it's early and has been so cold and wet. The White River bottom boosts a dark, rich loam. Other spots seem to be a more sandy soil. They grow a variety of grains and grasses here, much more than we did in Kentucky, since the land is better in larger areas.

We stopped at a farm tonight to ask if there was a creek nearby to camp at, and the couple insisted we park in their yard. They seem to be friendly enough, but I think they only invited us so we would buy grain and food from them. We've camped near several farms, and I must say these were the most insistent people we've met.

I said no to the wife's pie, but I did buy a round of cheese. She said it was made recently but needed a good week to ripen properly. I had to promise her we'd wait a few more days before we cut into it.

She was a snooper, too—wanted to see what we had in our wagons. I tried to be as polite as possible when she raised our wagon end flaps and lifted box lids. When she tried that with Mary's wagon, Nellie, who was inside the wagon, just "happened" to strongly tap her foot on the provisions box to slam the lid on the women's fingers. Nellie doesn't let anyone take advantage of her or her belongings. (She has been a good mother hen to have along on this trip.)

When the woman saw Mary's Kitty-Corner quilt blocks, she got all excited and invited us into her house to see the quilt top she had just put in the frame this week to quilt. The pattern was called the Indiana Puzzle, and it was the ugliest and poorest quilt I have ever seen. There was no color theme at all and very uneven stitching. Her long lazy stitches will snap the first time that quilt gets wet and heavy.

Later, when we were out of the woman's house, Mary suggested the woman had poor vision to give her the benefit of the doubt. Nellie added she must also be color-blind.

Ann has now decided to go ahead and quilt her Rose of Sharon top when we reach our destination. I told her that finishing that quilt before she was betrothed was courting disaster. She said she knows the superstition that if the quilt is finished too soon, the engagement—if she ever gets one—will be broken and she'll be doomed to spinsterhood forever. But as soon as we have a roof over our head, she wants to set up the quilting frame and stitch up her wedding quilt. Besides, she says, with all the bachelors we're seeing on the trail, she is sure she'll find one to marry soon. I'll keep you posted.

Enclosed is the pattern we saw today. Add it to your collection, but be sure to make the colors coordinate!

Collecting quilt patterns along the trail,

Deborah

Dear Betsy,

Our little camp has had to weather a late snowstorm. We haven't had any big snows in Kentucky the last few years, so this was almost a treat for the children. Emma and Valentine turned their faces to the sky and blinked with wonder when the flakes lit on their skin.

It started about two hours before we stopped to camp in the late afternoon and continued on and off, sometimes heavy, through the night. I looked out the back during the night when I heard wolves howling. With the big moon behind them, it was an eerie but beautiful sight to see their silhouettes up on the snowy hill. The storm has been miserable—for the cold it brought—but beautiful at the same time.

It's back to trying to keep everyone warm again. Children went to bed bundled up in their winter coats. Sacks were thrown over the chicken cage to cut out the cold wind. And the dogs curled up together near the fire. The snow was deep enough that the animals had to paw the ground to find grass this morning. Our breakfast of fried mush slices was sprinkled with the white stuff until it melted.

Flakes continued to fall for several hours as we forded the White River, again. It made conditions miserable for crossing, but at least the cold hardened the mud that has been giving us problems.

There were landings going up and down the banks, so I'm sure people cross it when the water level is down. With no ferry in the area, we had to make the crossing ourselves. James tried to get the horse to walk across the river, but it started swimming soon after it was off the bank and did not touch bottom until they reached the other side. He poked a long limb in several places to check the depth and decided it was too deep to raise the beds on blocks and pull the wagons through the water. The only option was to float everything across the river.

Everything had to be unloaded out of the wagons. The boys greased the tent and laid it out on the bank's edge. Using all the adults and older boys, we lifted the empty wagon bed off the running gear and set it on top of the tent. Wrapping the tent up the sides, we lashed it tight with ropes and filled the "boat" with part of the wagon's belongings. With oxen tied to each side of the wagon, and James and John on horseback leading the way, they pulled the bed into the water and swam it across onto the other side. The older boys rode in the bed and helped unload the belongings out onto the ground. Leaving those oxen on the other side of the river, the men and horses pulled the empty bed back to the other side. After warming up by the fire and resting, we repeated the process over and over until all the provisions, beds, running gear, animals, and children were on the opposite bank.

Mary's provision wagon was the first to go across. Nellie crossed over during the middle of the morning to start a campfire on the other side where the food and utensils were. She boiled coffee, heated food, and ferried it across to the rest of us on the other side when we needed warming up. Hoe cakes were devoured faster than Nellie could spread the batter on both the hoe and shovel. Hot fried meat pies were a welcome treat for supper tonight.

After everything was safely across, we had to put the wagons back together and reload everything. It took all day, starting at first morning light to campfire light, to move four wagons. If we have twenty to thirty wagons in our group, we would have been at this spot for days.

Our weariness was lifted tonight by the newest member of our family. John crossed the cow early this morning because he sensed she was ready to drop the calf. Sure enough, she had a little heifer tonight. Even though I think the cow would have liked to have been alone for the ordeal, the boys pitched her stake close to the fire and rigged up the tent for protection from the wind and cold. The new heifer has a white star on her brown face, so she was promptly named Snowflake by Sarah. Because she's so little on this cold trail, we'll have to make room for Snowflake to ride in a wagon for a few days.

Writing from snowy Indiana,

Deborah

Saturday afternoon, April 8, 1854
ready to cross the Wabash River

Dear Betsy,

Two days of waiting at this campsite has been a trial for us, to say the least. Due to the recent rains, there is a backup of wagons and families waiting to cross the Wabash River. People are getting restless and irritable because some have been here for several days. The river isn't real wide like the others we've had to ferry across, but the water level has been high and the current swift due to rains upstream. The tavern operator told John he's seen the river grow up to nine miles wide when it's flooded, so people shouldn't complain about a few days' wait. At least the rain has stopped and the temperature has warmed up a few degrees.

We've had time to explore Vincennes. Several brick and limestone buildings grace the town. Visiting the stores to compare prices from other towns has become a game.

The white spire of the huge red-bricked Catholic cathedral loomed above us because it is close to the river's edge. Ann and I paused to look at the four round Venetian glass windows above the doorway and decided to sneak in to view the interior. We quietly stole up to the beautiful white altar and said a prayer of thanks to God for getting us safely this far on our trip.

This town is the oldest settlement in Indiana and was the territorial capital for a while. It became a French trading post and military station after French missionaries made their way here over 150 years ago.

John tried his rusty French on two old men that were conversing in French while they sat outside a tavern. One rapidly fired back a question that stumped John. The man repeated in English, "How do you come to know that French dialect?" John told him he learned it from his French grandfather, who came to America from the province of Lorraine in France, to fight in the Revolution with Lafayette. That brought more questions of what battles did his grandfather fight in, and so on. It turns out this one man's father had been at the surrender of Cornwallis, too, so they had a good visit.

Even though John's grandfather died eighteen years ago, I can still hear his strong domineering French accent. A short man with a long face and flowing chestnut hair, he could still command attention from his family in his old age, just like he did his troops when he was a professional soldier.

Thinking of soldiers, we needed some last night to police our campground. After midnight we heard men yelling at each other, then firing guns. Apparently someone was drunk or mad, and decided to settle the matter with weapons. After the gunfire quit, I looked out the wagon to see what was going on. John and James crawled out their wagons, pulling their boots on as they tumbled out. Rifles in hand, they headed for the commotion. The boys scrambled into my wagon for protection when John left. I made sure the revolver was loaded and ready to fire if I needed to defend us. There was no more sleep in camp after that incident.

John later reported that one man lay dead when they got to the scene and the other person who apparently did the shooting was not in sight. A group of men searched wagons in hopes of finding the killer. Someone finally noticed a trail of blood from a wounded person. They followed it with a lighted torch down to the river's edge, where they lost the trail.

This morning, the widow and her family buried the man in the cemetery at Vincennes. She has two older boys, so I think they decided to stay with their wagon train and go on to their destination. The murderer was found. He confessed and was hung at noon. He should have been brought into the sheriff in town, but the train council that the families were traveling with made and carried out the decision. I pity the second wife, too. She's innocent of her husband's crime, but she'll be paying the price of his shame for the rest of her life. Two women's lives, and their children's, have been altered by the stupid drunk fighting of their men.

Our bell mare has been having problems, too. The tinkling of the bell around her neck always keeps our mules close by since she's their favorite. Now she has a new admirer from another camp. This one hobbled old mule just won't let her alone. The mare is on a forty-foot picket rope, set in the ground by a swivel ring. She goes round and around trying to stay clear of the beast, and he just hobbles as fast as he can to catch up with her. She finally gave him a swift kick that has slowed his romancing for a little while.

The boys took advantage of the wait and got out fish hooks and line. They cut down tree limbs for poles and spent the morning sitting on the bank, catching fish. Guess what they used for bait?! That cheese from the farmer's wife we were supposed to "let ripen" a few days! She knew it was going bad when she sold it to me. It was so rank that it was going into the river one way or another.

It must have made good bait, because by noon they had enough fish for our whole camp for dinner. I dipped the catfish in flour, butter, then cornmeal, and fried them in a hot skillet. We have to eat it carefully because of the bones, but it made a tasty meal. We ate the last of the sliced pickled potatoes we had along, and Ann's bread.

I wouldn't let the girls go down to the river since it is high, so we've kept them occupied with sewing projects. Sarah is quilting a flower design on a hot pad to use on the handles of the hot cooking pots.

Ann snagged her skirt getting out of the wagon recently and we both have burn holes around our hems, so George Ann sits next to us to practice her mending techniques on our skirts while Ann pieces quilt blocks and I write this letter. Our dresses will be in shambles by the end of the trip, so there is no need to worry about the girl's awkward stitching and her fat needle ruining them. She has to learn on something. George Ann tried to get Mary to sit still long enough to patch her skirt, but Valentine was wound up today and kept her on the run. She was ready to use hobbles on him to curtail his wanderings.

Trying to patiently wait our turn,

Deborah and family

Doctoring with Whiskey

late Sunday evening, April 9, 1854
camped on Embarras River in Illinois

Dear Betsy,

Roads were muddy going the eight miles into Lawrenceville today. We went past town to camp on the Embarras River to prepare for another river crossing.

As soon as we stopped, I dug out the medicine box. Besides Ann's worsening cough, the girls have come down with sniffles. A cup of catnip tea was given to all tonight to help the colds. Ann made a whiskey-sugar syrup for her cough. I hope she doesn't hack as much in bed tonight. It's been disturbing all of our sleep. Sarah complained of an earache, so John sat her in his lap and puffed tobacco smoke from his pipe into her ear, which seemed to warm it and ease the pain. I think quiet time in her father's arms helped just as much as the smoke.

Ann brewed her cup of hot chocolate she's been saving, but ended up giving it to a stranger instead. She thought another woman needed it more than she did. When we settled for the night, we parked our wagons near a young Swedish immigrant family. Wondering why the wife wasn't out cooking, Nellie went to investigate. Not finding her answer from the husband, who couldn't speak much English, she went to check on the woman when he motioned that his wife was lying in the wagon. Figuring out very quickly that the woman was in labor, Nellie and Mary moved right into the wagon—much to the relief of the distressed husband—and took charge of the woman's care. An hour ago she finally gave birth to a very quiet, small son. Since the woman seemed to be short on bedding, Mary wrapped the baby in an old

49

baby quilt that all her children had used. Ann gave her the cup of hot chocolate to help her regain her strength.

I pray the baby and woman live, since neither seem to be in the best of health. The Swedish couple have two other very young children who ended up eating with us and are now sleeping in Mary's wagon.

This Swede wasn't the first pregnant woman we've seen on the trail. I'm glad we're traveling between my pregnancies, for I usually have a child every couple of years. Young men are at their robust best as they travel to new land. In the meantime, their wives are sometimes very pregnant and taking care of a large brood of children.

I recently heard a man brag that his woman didn't have anything to do since they were traveling instead of toiling on their old homestead. By the looks of the poor overworked woman, her family, the wagon, and animals, I'd say he was lazy and neglecting their needs to boot. I don't condone violence, but I just wanted to hit him upside the head with a skillet to wake him up to his family's poor condition and knock some responsibility into his thick skull. We've seen all kinds of people on the road!

Doctoring with whiskey, chocolate, and prayers,

Deborah

Monday evening, April 10, 1854
camped on the Fox River

Dear Betsy,

Weather has warmed both the earth and our spirits today. This afternoon we could almost imagine a slight hint of green fuzz on the trees in the distance. The height and density of grass increases at each stop. I finally feel that spring will arrive.

Better weather, and an onion, has improved some of the family's colds. A fellow traveler gave me an onion, saying it was a surefire way to cure a cold. She recommended I cut up the onion and put it in a cup with a half-measure of sugar poured on top. Then I was to invert the cup on a saucer. In a couple of hours, as the onion juice filtered through the sugar, a thick syrup collected on the saucer. The women said to give each child a small half-teaspoonful of the juice. The mixture could also be used as a poultice for the congested chest. After spending the night in the enclosed wagon with three children who were literally breathing onions with every breath, I think all our heads were opened up for the rest of the trip! Tonight I think we're all going to start sleeping in the tent where there is more fresh air.

Today we crossed the Fox River by Olney and paused here for the night. At twenty miles, this is the longest distance we have traveled so far in a day. With drier weather and flatter roads, the men hope we can pick up our pace and make better time than we've done through the last two states.

Tomorrow we head ten miles to the Big Muddy Creek and follow it south to where it meets the Little Wabash River. People suggested we use the crossing there. The Big Muddy Creek is small but deep, so it was advised to go the few extra miles to cross once at the Little Wabash, rather than twice.

The soil here is a dark rich loam. Even when it is slightly wet, you can squeeze a handful of it and it is still slightly crumbly. Our Kentucky red clay is so poor compared to it. New alfalfa and young wheat are so lush-looking here that we've had problems keeping our herd out of the farmers' fields.

Out of a more than mild curiosity, John asked a farmer what land sells for around here. We were shocked when he said around fifteen to thirty dollars per acre. Top established farms could go as high as sixty dollars per acre! With prices like that, we can only hope that land in Kansas, selling for around a dollar an acre, is half as good as this. I wonder what kind of country we are running into.

Trying to make up time on the road,

Deborah

Wednesday evening, April 12, 1854
camped on the prairie

Dear Betsy,

We've been on the road almost a month. When I'm trudging along the trail daydreaming, I'm back in Kentucky walking up Slate Creek to Owingsville until something snaps my attention back to the present. I wish I could say it seems like we just left Kentucky yesterday, but instead it seems like we've been on the trail and in limbo forever. Since there is no turning back, I wish we could cross the next hill and see our final destination at the bottom of it. I wonder when that will be.

Today we went eighteen miles before stopping for the night. There was no creek or farmstead in sight, so we had to use the water we carry in kegs with us for such an emergency. The animals drank most of it, but I saved a little for cooking and washing for ourselves. In the morning the ground will be covered with dew, so the herd will get their water from the wet grass. We'll stop at the first sight of water tomorrow to fill up the animals and the kegs.

We watched the most beautiful sunset tonight as we walked our final mile. The billowing clouds in an array of purple, pink, yellow, and blue kept my thoughts off my weary legs. It was spectacular and mesmerizing. We just kept walking to the horizon until the haloed sun sank off the earth's surface. Gleaming stars twinkled in the sky as pale dusk settled on our camp. As long as we see nature's wonderful displays now and then, we can put up with the occasional bad weather.

We are beginning to see why Illinois is called the Prairie State. Timber and civilization has thinned out to vast stretches of grass. It is amazing to see so far from the flat ground. There is an openness that is hard to explain. Ann is feeling almost threatened—unprotected without the closeness of trees and hills wrapped around her. John, on the other hand, seems to breathe easier; he's almost glad to have things open around him. I can't say I feel either way. I'm just concerned about taking care of the family, no matter what terrain we're in.

Someone spoke of you today. Were your ears burning? I made rice pudding and served it without tasting it first. It was soupy with hard kernels since it hadn't cooked long enough. Nellie laughed and piped up that it tasted just like yours! (You will never live down the story that as a young bride you hastily served company rice pudding without sampling it for doneness, and then you pretended it was the way you liked it instead of putting it back on the fire to cook longer.) We need a good laugh to keep our spirits up, so I hope you don't mind it was at your expense. Believe me, we really miss you, and your cooking!

Writing about cooking problems, our plans to have light bread along with our noon meal today were foiled by Blackie. Yesterday morning I mixed and kneaded bread to bake in the evening when we arrived at our campsite. The constant motion of the wagon during the day causes the bread to rise real nice and be ready to bake in the Dutch oven when we camp at night. Well, we got into camp very late, so I fixed hoecakes for supper and baked the bread for the next day instead. It was late, and in my hurry to get to bed I left the bread out to cool on the end gate instead of putting it away in the wagon. Just as I was crawling into the tent, I heard the clatter of pans off the back of the wagon, and then Blackie streaked past the firelight with the loaf in his mouth.

There was no way I could catch him in the dark before the loaf was gobbled up. I didn't know whether to laugh or cry. The thought of his trick was funny, but at the same time it takes work and supplies to feed our family, and I don't have much of either to spare. Some nights I'm so tired, I don't have the energy to yell at child or beast. But I guess I still need a chuckle now and then.

Laughing at tonight's cooking failure,

Deborah

Sunday afternoon, April 16, 1854
on the Shoal Creek

Dear Betsy,

It was pitch dark when got to the Kaskaski River Friday night, so we committed the sin of staying on the east side, hoping rains didn't come up during the night to hamper our crossing. Since it had sprinkled lightly off and on all afternoon, we traveled late trying to find the river and get across before dark. We must have traveled over twenty miles after we left Salem. There was a heavy, cloudy sky with no moon, and we were yelling back and forth between the wagons to keep everyone together. It was so different from nights when the sky is clear and you can see your shadow. Weather can change very fast here, it seems.

Crossing the river took the better part of Saturday. We had to float and swim everything across. I thought we were going to lose one of the mules in the water this time. It slipped in a hole while crossing and went under for a moment. You know how fast a mule can panic and drown when it gets water in its ears. Luckily, the mule was tied in line with the horses, who kept tugging it up until they got to the opposite shore.

The boys put Snowflake in the wagon when it crossed so there wasn't a danger of losing her. All the children have become so attached to her that she's their pet. She doesn't care who is giving her attention as long as she gets it. I think poor Blackie feels like a new "puppy" has replaced him. We've had offers to sell Snowflake along the way, but it would break the children's hearts to part with her now.

Yesterday we went on a few miles after the crossing and camped on the Shoal Creek for our Sunday break. It turned out to be a good area to camp. Ann found wild onions and tender new dandelion leaves along the bank to add to the soup pot of beans and bacon.

There is a tree on the creek with a grapevine hanging from its limbs. It didn't have the thick cover of leaves, so we could follow the vine from the base all the way up to a high limb. It had one thick loop of vine hanging loose enough for the children to swing on. I wish we could have timed it to be here when the

55

grapes were plumb and ready to be picked. The thought of a fried pie of fresh grapes makes my mouth water.

Right now we're relaxing under the shade of the wagon as we digest our noon meal. John and James scared up a flock of prairie grouse this morning when they were out hunting and bagged four of the birds. We usually make a large, long fire so both families can cook together, so we put all four birds on the spittle and the girls took turns rotating them. We roasted the birds to a golden crisp until the meat was starting to fall off the bones. The tantalizing smell kept everyone around the fire, waiting for the meal to be ready. We enjoyed every delectable morsel. The grouse had a wild taste to them compared to young chickens, but it was so good to eat something besides bacon!

Enjoying a Sunday picnic today,

Deborah

Monday evening, April 17, 1854
west of Lebanon, Illinois

Dear Betsy,

We holed up in the general store in Lebanon for a while this afternoon during a thunderstorm. When hail started to drop, we scooted the little children under cover of a real roof. The men walked on since they couldn't leave the stock and wagons. The animals were tense with the rumbling storm and the men wanted to get them out of town before the herd stampeded and caused trouble. We knew what direction they were going, so we decided to wait out the worst of the storm and catch up with them later.

Got in on a little local propaganda talk while we were waiting. The storekeeper asked where we were from, since he didn't know us, and where were we headed. He boasted a little about the town, adding that they need settlers in the area. They even have a school, the McKendree College, for our youngsters when they reach that age. Although we probably never would be able to pay for it, I would love for the children to go to school. Did you have that dream for us children?

The storm died down just as fast as it blew up, so the road didn't get very wet. We've had beautiful weather this week except for this one storm.

When we strolled down the trail to catch up with the wagons, a farmer was plowing his field with a double team of oxen. Apparently he knew the storm wasn't one to last long because he didn't even stop his work. We've been running into a few scattered homesteads now as we get closer to St. Louis. It is smooth, flat land here. It lays so open and exposed compared to the rolling hills of Kentucky.

It was easy to find where the men camped. We just followed a trail of thread. Sarah spied the empty wooden spool first, then the end of the white thread that apparently came off the spool. I wrapped the thread back on the spool to reclaim it, and we followed it to within sight of the wagons. It wasn't quite a full spool, but I must have rewound a good 100 yards. We later figured out that in our haste to take cover in Lebanon, Nellie dislodged her sewing basket when she climbed off the wagon seat. Evidently the spool popped out when the wagon hit a bump, but the thread got caught on the wicker lip of the basket. The spool of thread unraveled itself as the party traveled on. At the price of thread, Nellie was grateful that Sarah spied it along our trail.

Following the trail of thread,

Deborah

Wednesday evening, April 19, 1854
East St. Louis, Illinois

Dear Betsy,

Yesterday we crossed the Silver Creek and traveled eighteen miles to East St. Louis on the Mississippi River. Today we looked around town, then moved upriver to get away from the crowds. Above St. Louis there are a few snags near the bank that the boats avoided, so they aren't stopping right along the shoreline in front of us. Sandbanks were present but seemed high, stable, and easy for the traffic to get around.

I wish you could be here to see this sight. The Mississippi River is like a busy highway, only using water as its road. I think it is wider than all the rivers we have crossed combined! I worry it will test my fear of crossing to the maximum, but it's a fear I have to face, or otherwise stay behind.

White steamboats with gingerbread trim, smoke belching from their fire stacks, and water swishing through their stern wheels paddle up and down the wide river. People standing on the decks are staring back at us on the shore staring at them. Men hefting box after box up the gangplanks of waiting vessels crowd the shoreline at the landing. Crude log rafts stacked precariously high with boxes, barges being used as ferries, and wooden and bark canoes dot the waters up and downstream.

I can imagine the awe of the first explorers when they saw this region. It must have been beautiful back then. We've always heard about Lewis and Clark starting their exploration of the West from here, but think of all the fur trappers who explored this area first. Those men would probably be sad to see how the tranquil banks of the river have changed over the years.

We couldn't resist seeing the town, so we took turns with James and Mary. Since we're camped on the East St. Louis side, we took a passenger ferry across to see the main town of St. Louis. (With this much activity, one of the men has to stay with our camp at all times. Nellie and Ann were not going to be left behind this time to take care of things!)

It's hard to describe such a bustling place as St. Louis, once called the City of the French. Besides the immense population of the town, a third of it now German, there are thousands of travelers from all walks and nationalities here, stocking up to head West. We heard so many types of languages on the boardwalks that we lost count.

Stores sold everything imaginable and then some. We even saw several businesses advertising that they bought and sold slaves. There is a big market for excess Missouri slaves to be shipped downriver to Memphis and New Orleans. I just can't imagine it being considered a respectable business, but they sure do advertise!

Hordes of people from Back East take the train to St. Louis. At this time there is no train that goes on to Independence, Missouri, so everyone must either board a boat to go up the Missouri River, or take the overland road. Some actually buy supplies and outfit wagons here and load them onto the boats with them. I guess they think the prices are cheaper here than the last town on the edge of the frontier, where they get off the boat. We priced the boat charges ourselves, but decided that with the herd and stopping at Tipton's, it was best we stay on the trail. The thought of sitting on a boat for a week or so instead of walking across the state definitely had its appeal, though.

When we inquired about the ferry crossing, we found out we have two options. We can cross the Mississippi River here at St. Louis, but then we would have to cross the Missouri River at St. Charles. The other option is to follow the river up to Alton and cross there instead. That way we can go between the Mississippi and Missouri Rivers and not have to cross the Missouri River until we leave Boone County, Missouri, and head west for Kansas.

I'll send a group of letters to you from here. Who knows what town in Missouri I'll be able to send my letters from next.

Awed by the big city,

Deborah

Thursday afternoon, April 20, 1854
Alton, Illinois

Dear Betsy,

Today we're camped upriver near Alton, which is a fascinating, industrious town. Alton Harbor, a major shipping point along the Mississippi River, has over a thousand steamboat landings in its waters. Many steamboat captains have built mansions on top of the hills to view the river.

At a townsman's suggestion, we went up to see the monster on the limestone bluffs near the river. It's a faded painting of a bird—or animal—with scales, antlers, wings, and a tail. I guess it has been on the bluffs for hundreds of years. The Indians called the creature the *Piasa*, meaning the bird that devours men, and they have a legend that goes with it. This monster was strange enough to give a person nightmares.

The water is clear here, not brownish like I thought it might be. We've done wash and hung things out to dry in today's brilliant sunshine. We hung bedding out to air, too. The wagons were getting stale and moldy-smelling from the damp bedrolls.

Women around each campfire are doing extra baking while we all have the chance. Seems like everyone has a different version than the next for what they fix. We're trying to bake and dry enough bread to last us the next week on the road.

We've visited among our fellow travelers to see where they were from originally, and where they are headed. Their answers varied, depending on their husbands' dreams, much like our men. Some women were excited about just starting out; others had been on the trail for weeks, like us. There are several immigrant women that speak different languages than we do. They struggled to communicate with us, as if they hungered for companionship. It's like these women think we know the answers to life on the trail because we're American. I'm afraid they are going to have to find out like we did—by trial and error.

Travelers from Back East, especially Ohio, are leaving their states because of drought problems on their land. Hard times cause the men to pull up stakes and try their hand elsewhere. Talked to some people heading for the Kansas Territory, too. One

61

group had several wagons of black people traveling with them, so I knew they were from the South. The woman asked if we were going to be on the free-state or slavery side. When I told her my view, I got laughed at. She said I couldn't be a free-state woman with a Southern accent like mine—people would never believe me. I hope whomever we settle next to in Kansas has a more open mind than that prejudiced woman.

For meals today, I've fixed every Northern recipe I had learned from a New England woman I met last week, just to see that Mississippian get riled.

I think this woman met her Northern match this evening, though. The lady from Mississippi and another from Boston, were arguing about Harriet Beecher Stowe's *Uncle Tom's Cabin*. The book came out two years ago, and it is about the treatment of slaves. The author was determined to awaken the North to the wickedness of slavery and she succeeded in riling both sides of the Union. The womens' husbands finally stepped in and got them separated before it came to blows. I remember reading that book. Some of the story was right on the mark about the slaves but other parts were embellished, in my opinion.

I did feel sorry for one woman from the South I met yesterday. Her family had taken the train into St. Louis with the purpose of heading on and starting a new plantation in Oregon. She was now faced with the daunting job of living out of a wagon for the next several months as they headed West. The poor lady had left her cook back home and didn't even know how to boil water. Being raised a Southern lady on a big plantation, she was entirely out of her element and beginning to panic. She finally found her voice today and screamed at her husband, "I came all this distance for this?!?" I fear the husband will have a wild, mad wife on the trail. I hope the woman doesn't go insane before they reach their destination.

Sympathizing with other women on the trail,

Deborah

Warm Milk and Mud

Saturday evening, April 22, 1854
in Missouri

Dear Betsy,

It's a calm, still night, except for an occasional hoot of a nearby owl. With the moon so bright, I could almost write this letter without the aid of the lantern. The river is a glistening band of silver in the moonlight, with tiny dots of stars sparkling on the surface. Campfires glow up and down the rivers across from us tonight like little torches of bright yellow. Some woman probably saw our campfire last night when we were one of the throng staked out along the river's edge and thought the same things. I didn't realize there were so many wagon trains heading for Alton until we got out of the congestion. Tonight, as I stare across the river we crossed today, I feel a sense of relief that the crossing is over, but also resignation that we're in Missouri, another state farther away from Kentucky. I feel another wave of homesickness hit and try to swallow my regret. Tears will only ruin the words I write and bring me no satisfaction. I concentrate through the campground noises to the lapping of the water on the edge of the bank. It calms my nerves for now.

We woke up this morning in an alien world blocked off from civilization by a fog as thick as pea soup. Our bedding was heavy with moisture. Last night's fire was a bank of soggy, cold coals. The fog was so thick that we didn't realize it was our turn to cross the river until we were right up to the huge ferry. At least I didn't have time to panic. Our view of the river was blocked by a thick, low, white mist. It was like a dizzying curtain—only a few yards high but opaque and moving, never letting us peek through the window of our morning world. Going across the river felt like we were on an island floating in space. We had no sense of depth, width, direction, or time.

We bore the brunt of the cost and ferried everything across, wagons and animals. This ferry, actually more like a barge, was big enough to carry all four wagons, both families, and all the animals at one time. This river was too wide for us to chance swimming the herd across. In the case of this morning's weather, they could have swum around for hours before finding the bank.

About the time we got everything unloaded, the fog lifted, and we could see what we missed. There was so much traffic on the water it's a wonder we weren't hit by a paddleboat in midstream! Maybe because the captains are high up in the pilothouse, they could see above the fog. I'm just glad we are all accounted for on the Missouri side of the Mississippi River.

We traveled a few miles this afternoon between the bends of the Mississippi and Missouri Rivers before we stopped for the night. The men thought getting the animals on the trail after their ferry ride would get them back into their routine and calm them down. We've had some problems with the animals in the crowded camp grounds, and it's just easier to keep track of them in smaller areas. With so many people heading toward the West, though, I think we'll always have someone camping near us for the rest of the trip. And I thought we'd be on a lonely deserted trail to Kansas. Was I ever wrong!

On the crowded road to new land,

Deborah

Monday evening, April 24, 1854
camped near Warrenton, Missouri

Dear Betsy,

For the last two days we've been traveling between the rivers on a ridge that runs along the top of a bluff overlooking the Missouri River Valley to the south of us. It's been pretty scenery with trees bursting with fresh new leaves and lush grass. We've been warned that this Boone's Lick Road can get very rough and rutted in places, but it hasn't been any worse than other parts of our trail from Kentucky.

Daytime temperatures are just right—not cold enough to require coats, but not hot enough to sweat. The nights are still cool enough that you want to snuggle down in the covers, but we're comfortable in the tent.

We traveled yesterday since we had paused for several days by the Mississippi River. Stopped at St. Charles for noon, then paid a two-bit per wagon toll to travel the ten-mile plank road that goes as far as the settlement of Cottleville. Bad weather and the overflow of creeks can make this stretch difficult, so the ingenious idea of laying split trees on the trail took place a few years ago. In several places, though, we hit bad places where the wood had been removed. Someone probably stole it for firewood or lumber.

Last night we camped in a protected cove facing the Missouri River. Water seeped down the sides of the bluffs behind us. It was one of the best camp sites we've had on this trip until we woke up to a putrid smell. Apparently Blackie surprised a skunk and got sprayed. All day long the poor dog would run up to a child to be petted and they would scream and run away from him instead. Our eyes watered all day from the odor that followed us down the trail.

The boys are running up to me now with a rabbit one of them just shot. John said they could take turns practicing their shooting with the rifle. By the proud look on James Monroe's face, I'd say he was my lucky provider for tonight's supper. I hope we can find wild game along the route to supplement our dwindling meat supply. Any change from salted bacon helps everyone's spirits and appetite.

They also gave me a piece of paper Jimmy had spied flapping in the breeze. He found it stuck on the end of a stick at the edge of the road. A message was scribbled on a page torn from a journal. Left by a family that camped in this very spot last night, it described the markings of their young dog, named Tippy. It disappeared during the night and could not be found when they left camp this morning.

I think supper will be delayed because nine kids have scattered to look for the poor puppy. He'll probably be scared out of his wits and hide from them if he is still in the area. I told the children it's possible the dog caught up with his family during the day, but they were sure it was still in the area and needed help.

Another busy day with dogs and children,

Deborah

Dear Betsy,

We've become accustomed to the trail and forget that danger and accidents can happen at any time. Everyone is okay, but we had some scares.

The children seem to have forgotten the incident. They found the old Graham Cave they heard about behind an abandoned log cabin and coerced John into lighting a torch and going inside with them. I can't curtail their adventures, but I can sure worry about them, just the same.

Belvard got hot and tired of walking beside the oxen today and he hopped up on the wagon tongue and sat sideways on the tongue between the oxen's heels and the wagon wheels for a while. John and the boys have done this numerous times and I didn't think anything of it at the time.

An hour later I hear George Ann scream from the wagon behind me. Running back, I didn't see her at first, but then I spied her face down underneath the wagon, her skirt pinned under a wheel. James Monroe's face was ashen as he tried to hold the oxen from moving the wagon farther. Crawling on my stomach underneath the wagon from behind, I tugged at her dress and prayed she wasn't run over. I was so frightened that I ripped the bunched layers of skirt in half. Luckily, just her dress was under the wagon, but she had a lump the size of an egg on the back of her head and scrapes on her face and arms. George Ann had tried to jump on the wagon tongue like Belvard had, but she tripped on her long skirt, fell between the wheels, and hit her head on the wagon box going under. Of course James Monroe felt responsible for his little sister since he was in charge of the wagon. I couldn't talk afterwards. They both learned a very serious lesson that didn't need an added lecture from me.

After doctoring up George Ann's sores, she spent the rest of the day in the wagon. She's going to ache all over for a few days. At least she has company in the wagon to keep her mind off her problems. Yes, we found Tippy. The scruffy brown and white puppy must have been attacked by some bigger animal, probably a prairie wolf, and has a lame back leg. The boys patched him up and put him in the wagon to recuperate.

Mary's Johnny got in her medicine bag yesterday and drank a large portion of laudanum. She poured enough milk and water down his throat to make him vomit, which got most of the medicine out of him. He was a very sick boy for a while. Mary stayed up with him all night to make sure he didn't slip into a coma. If Jimmy hadn't seen his brother play with the bottle and reported it right away, Johnny would have drifted off to sleep, never to wake up. The medicine that Mary may need desperately farther down the trail to cure her sick children almost killed one of them instead.

It dawned on me that if one of these accidents had been fatal, we would have been using those extra boards on the side of the wagon for a burial today. Out here in the middle of nowhere, there is no town or doctor nearby to help us. It will be the same thing wherever we settle in Kansas.

Oh Betsy, I'm just sick to think we could have lost two children in less than twenty-four hours.

Worrying about accidents on the trail,

Deborah and Mary

Thursday evening, April 27, 1854
Columbia, Missouri

Dear Betsy,

We're getting near Albert Tipton's place, since his letter said he lived northwest of Columbia. If we can put in a full day's travel from our camping spot here east of Columbia, we should be with family tomorrow tonight. Mary and Nellie are getting anxious to see their brother and his family again. They left so many years ago, I hardly remember them. There is so much about Albert and Sallie that I do not know. For example, is Sallie a good cook? What quilt pattern is she working on this year? Is Albert still blacksmithing? Why did they decide to leave Boone County? I don't think they have any slaves, but what is their view on the settling of Kansas as a free state? We'll have time enough on the road together to find out their opinions.

I wonder what their homestead is like. Will it be a well-kept place with a decent stand of orchard trees, or a shanty on the edge of a creek bank?

On this stretch of road we've passed by a few farms, mostly along the river bottoms, as we dip up and down the hills along the trail. The hills here are small, though, compared to Kentucky. Homesteads are more primitive and wild-looking compared to the manicured fields of Illinois. Slave shacks in the farmyards are prominent again, something we haven't seen since we left Kentucky.

Trees are only seen along the creeks now. The healthy prairie grass seems to expand to the horizon. It's already a foot tall. It is very different from the variety of grasses that grow in Kentucky.

Ran into a little storm today. Dust was blowing so bad after nooning that we wore handkerchiefs over our faces to keep from eating so much of the stuff. Threatening clouds billowed up in the east, but then the wind changed direction and the temperature cooled considerably. Instead of a good thunderstorm, the wind died down and we experienced a short, gentle shower that settled the dust on the trail and our faces. I think I shook a half-bushel of dirt from our clothes tonight when we got ready for bed.

69

Last night we camped north of Fulton. I think we traveled a good eighteen miles before stopping for the night. It was dark enough that we had problems pitching the tent.

Darkness works better, though, to find bugs for the chickens. Now that it has warmed up, the children look for insects and worms to supplement the chickens' diet. One boy holds the lantern, one rolls the log or other debris over on the ground, and the other children snatch the insects and put them in a jar to smother them overnight. I've been amazed at what they have found. At least it is one chore they do without being asked. The chickens look forward to their tasty snacks bright and early in the morning. I suggested to the boys that they could start collecting the crickets that find their way under our bedrolls at night, too.

I hope I can let the chickens roam free at Albert's for the few days we are there. I'm sure they could use a rest from their jolting ride on the back of the wagon. Maybe Sallie will have some new young poults that I can take along since my hens haven't had a chance to hatch their own broods this spring.

Speculating about the Tiptons and the chickens,

Deborah

Sunday evening, April 30, 1854
Boone County, Missouri

Dear Betsy,

It was so good to hear from you! When we got to Tipton's Friday, Sallie pulled out a letter addressed to us, in care of Albert. Tears welled in my eyes when I recognized your handwriting. You have no idea what a sense of relief I felt in knowing someone from home missed us.

Since you wrote and mailed the letter in early February, right after I told you we were moving, Albert got your letter before they knew we were coming. Sallie has been anxiously waiting ever since, not knowing who of all the families were coming, or even when to expect our arrival. The letter Mary sent to Albert in March explained it all, but they had a month of anticipation because of the letter you sent before we left home.

It is good to see Sallie and Albert again. Their son, Samuel Barnett, who was born right before they left Kentucky, is now almost eighteen years old. He looks like his father. They never did have any more children.

We've visited with other relations that live in the area, for several Tipton families moved here in the '30s. Remember Betsy Tipton that married Aaron Cornelison about a year before John and I married? They live nearby, too. I mistook children for their elders since I hadn't seen most of them in twenty years. Although bashful at first, our children were soon playing hide-in-seek with the Cornelison clan.

It's so good to have a decent meal from a kitchen, fresh produce from the garden, and good clean well water again!

Ann has whipped up some mouth-watering meals in Sallie's kitchen, much to the delight of all of us eating it. Sallie gave her the run of the cellar since she needs to finish cleaning it out before we move on. We've had fresh chicken and a garden salad with every noon meal. I'm sure glad Sally went ahead and put some garden in this spring!

While Sallie is preparing to leave with us, we women of the trail have been washing and airing out everything we can. Clothes and blankets were hung out in the sunshine from every line, tree, and bush on the place. Our wagons were smelling very stale and musty, so this will help make the rest of the trip more pleasant. I swept out several inches of dried mud from the floor of each wagon and found the thimble and some hair pins I had lost. Now everything is repacked and ready to go.

I scrubbed each of the children in a tub of hot soapy water, too. Everyone's hair was a tangled mess, so shampoos and haircuts were also in order. I soaked in the warm heavenly bath until my skin was wrinkled. I think that twenty minutes was the best part of our whole stop.

John and James have been repairing wagon wheels and the like. Two of our wheels had become loose the last few days and had to be reset. John had put wooden wedges between the metal rim and wooden wheel, but that was just a temporary repair. Last week James had to take a wheel off and soak it in a creek to make the wood swell enough to hold together to get here.

Albert is still blacksmithing, so he has shod some of our animals. Everything we needed to repair while we were still in civilization had to be done this weekend.

Tomorrow we start back on the trail. In a few weeks, I hope to finally be settled on our new land.

Glad for the stop, looking forward to tomorrow,

Deborah

Monday evening, May 1, 1854
site of Old Franklin, Missouri

Dear Betsy,

We're back on the road again, and as usual, waiting to cross another river. We left Albert's farm early this morning and headed southwest to get back on the Boone's Lick Road. With six wagons now in our group and the new oxen getting used to the trail, we're not traveling at our usual pace.

Sallie complained about being tired from the walk so far, and we just smiled, remembering the same feeling when we started out seven weeks ago. At least now we have warm weather and not six inches of frozen mud around our hems hitting our ankles with each step. Sallie has spent most of her time walking with her sisters-in-law, catching up on family news from Kentucky. I know Sallie hated to leave her nice home in Boone County, but she's putting on a brave front since the rest of us have already made the sacrifice.

Albert and Samuel are each watching a wagon. Their animals mixed in with our herd. Since we only have a few weeks of travel to Kansas, they have brought along a small herd of swine. So far they have traveled just as well as the cows.

Tonight we camped on the north side of the Missouri River by the foundation ruins of the Old Franklin townsite. It got flooded out years ago, so they relocated the town about two miles north of the river and renamed it New Franklin. Boonville, built directly across the river on a bluff, has become the flourishing river town of this area now.

As I write to you, I'm watching the steamboats cautiously navigating the snags and shifting sandbars up and downriver. The Missouri River has a completely different personality than the other rivers we've camped by. It's a swift, restless river that continually changes its crumbling perpendicular banks. Sand and logs are piled up along the bank from past floods. Broken trees stuck in the channels lie waiting to punch a hole in the hull and sink a boat. I'm not looking forward to this crossing.

The thickness and muddiness of the Missouri River water is beyond description. I don't think you could see an egg in the bottom of a glass of this ashen yellow water. We have to put a handkerchief over the mouth of each cup to keep from drinking dirt with the murky water. The quick bread we made tonight with the river water had a definite grittiness to it.

The cattle even paused a minute to sniff the water before their thirst overcame their worry about the smell. Do they know something that we don't?

Wondering about the water,

Deborah

Dear Betsy,

Went by Boone's Lick where Daniel Boone's sons boiled briny water from the springs to mine salt at the turn of the century. This road we're on was originally built to get to this salt lick.

About got seasick crossing the Missouri River yesterday. I swear the ferry slid up and down the current so much I thought we were going to spin a few circles in the middle of the trip. We were all green and woozy by the time we touched solid ground again. At least with this hazardous crossing and everyone being under the weather the past few days, I haven't had to do much cooking.

We traveled on to Arrow Rock last night to get decent water from the town's well. One old-timer we met there said that Boone's Lick Road now merges with the Santa Fe Trail. (The man that blazed the Santa Fe was from Old Franklin, where we camped last night.) He told the boys stories about how he traveled with the first caravan that left Arrow Rock on the old Osage Trace Trail for Santa Fe back in '22. I'm not sure I believed all his stories about Indian attacks and getting water from a buffalo, but he sure got the boys watching for both on the trail now.

Went only thirteen miles to Marshall today, and each step was torture. John kept pushing us on even though I think he was the sickest. I don't know if he didn't want to delay our progress, or he was trying to get to a town with a doctor before he collapsed.

Bad water, I assume from the river, has made us all sick with diarrhea. None of us felt like walking, but it was worse riding in the bumpy wagon. Besides, we had to stop so often to relieve our misery that it was impractical to jump in and out of the wagon each time. We have drunk all kinds of water on the trail and haven't been affected like this before. Ann and John are the worst of our group. The children aren't in quite as bad shape since they opted for warm milk instead of the "nasty" water, as they put it. I doled out limited quantities of laudanum to relieve all our discomfort.

Would you believe Mary's Johnny, who overdosed on the medicine, is not having any problems? He's skipping along the road happy as a lark. I guess he has enough laudanum in his system to protect him for life!

A bland meal of tea and hardtack is the only food I am giving the family for a few days to clean out everyone's intestines. That should save on our food supply this week!

I just overheard the boys talking about the bloated dead cow they saw in the river stuck in a logjam upstream of our camp the other day. Now I know what made us sick this week! I should have been boiling the water or at least stirred a piece of alum in our drinking water to purify it.

Sick on the trail,

Deborah

Thursday evening, May 4, 1854
Grand Pass, Missouri

Dear Betsy,

Camped by the river near Grand Pass. Weather has turned hot this week. This morning it was muggy when we got up and got worse as temperatures rose quickly before noon. Last night's rain shower made the humidity unbearable. Without a breeze to cool us off, we perspired to the point that it looked like we had poured water on our clothing. It has been a miserable day for man and beast. After John checked out the water depth in the river, we all took a cooling dip. Sunstroke came to mind, for we were walking all day in the hot sun and have been poorly lately because of dehydration and bad water.

Having problems with overheating and sores on some of the oxen. We've been rotating the extra pair to give the teams a break, but time is taking a toll on the animals. Two oxen have such sores on their necks under the yoke that John has been rubbing grease on the spots when we stop for the night. It crusts over and seems to protect the sores. Today he tied a piece of bacon rind under the yoke to protect one bad wound. Horseflies are beginning to be a problem for the animals. We've been blowing calomel into the animals' wounds to kill the fly eggs and try to break the cycle.

I've been doctoring children, too. The girls got into poison ivy the other day and have been driving themselves, and me, insane with their itching. Their faces are so puffed and red that they can hardly see. I've tried about every mixture of salve I can think of to ease their pain. A traveler suggested the girls drink plantain-leaf tea and gave me a few dried leaves of the plant from their medicine box. It seemed to help the girls sleep through the night better.

For the rest of us, I'm burning molasses and cornmeal in the skillet until crisp, then crumbling and brewing it for our hot brew. We're out of coffee beans until we do some trading. With the first month on the trail so cold, we drank more coffee than I thought we would.

Some provisions have held out well, and others we need to replenish before we cross into the new territory. Not knowing what we're getting into when we hit Kansas or how near a store we will be, will probably make me want to overstock everything I can think of and can afford so my children don't go hungry this fall.

It has helped immensely to have the cow and chickens along. Not only has the milk and eggs been a blessing to our diet, but I've also been able to trade them to other travelers who hunger for butter to put on their bread. We have certainly fared better than many families because I insisted a few of my chickens make the trip with us.

Snowflake is growing and having no problems keeping up with us. The hardest part is sharing the milk with this hungry heifer, although the children are ready to quit drinking milk "so Snowflake will grow big and strong." They are all complaining about drinking warm milk straight from the cow. I don't blame them. Now that the weather is warm, I tend to gag on it, too. We don't have time or a place to cool the milk before we drink it for our quick breakfast. I miss our springhouse in Kentucky that chilled the milk to icy cold.

Sometimes I read passages of my letters to you to the children. They like to help think up my closing line. Tonight during supper, James Monroe suggested the ending for today's letter. He caught Sarah making a depression in the mud and pouring her milk into it to let the dog lap up the evidence so she didn't have to drink it herself. I think that about sums up all our feelings.

Tired of warm milk and mud,

Deborah and children

Sunday afternoon, May 7, 1854
south side of Missouri River

Dear Betsy,

We're camped on the south bank of the Missouri River, right below old Fort Osage. Before breakfast this morning, I climbed up to the outpost site and watched the sun rise. At about a hundred feet above the water level I had a wide, open view of the opening colors of the day, and of the river below. Sometimes I need quiet times to myself—like this morning—to help me keep my sanity on this trip. It seems like I'm needing more of these breaks as the heat and tempers rise.

Filled up the water kegs at Lexington yesterday so we don't have to drink the river water. Not everyone is at full recovery yet, but all are feeling better. I hope that stopping for a day's rest will improve everyone's health and disposition.

It's unseasonably hot for this time of year. I think I could fry an egg in the skillet without starting a fire. Appetites are down, but thirst is up. I've kept a keg, wrapped in old sacks, full of tea to quench our thirst. When we stop by water, I unhook it from the back of the wagon and plunge the keg in the stream to cool it down. Some days we've had almost boiling tea by the time we stopped for the evening.

If we have enough water to spare, I splash water directly on my dress to cool off. It gives some relief while the moisture evaporates. Dipping bare feet in a cool stream at the end of the day also does wonders.

To compensate for the sultry heat, we've been leaving camp very early in the morning, then taking a longer noon break. When the day starts to cool down, about three, we push on for the rest of the day's mileage. Days are longer now, so we can travel later in the evening than when we started out.

When I went to hang up the washing today, I found the back of George Ann's dress had ripped. The material was getting thin from being outside in the sun and regular wear, and it just disintegrated. Of course it was a hand-me-down, so it wasn't new material to start with. All our clothing is in dire shape from this trip. When we're not filmed in dust, we're caked in mud and

79

manure. Washing in dirty water most of the time doesn't really get the clothes clean.

Things have gotten a little testy on the trail this week. Everyone is getting tired of being sick, hot and still on the road. Newly hatched mosquitoes and flies along the river bottom are driving both man and beast insane with itch.

John exploded after the boys let a mule wander off when they were supposed to be watching the herd. We were delayed two hours while the men hunted for the critter. Supper was not a pleasant affair yesterday.

And Blackie got bold and tried to steal Nellie's bread last night since he got away with that stunt with me once. She took after him screaming at the top of her lungs and pounding a spoon on a pan as she ran. That dog was so traumatized by her chase that he stayed away from the camp until Nellie went to bed.

Today I tried to soothe everyone's nerves by fixing extras-pecial meals. We're all tired of beans, bacon, and quick bread (covered with mosquitoes stuck on the crust). Breakfast was flapjacks with hot sorghum molasses and butter drizzled on top. Dinner's surprise was the last of the pickles and a dried-cherry pie.

This afternoon's drink of lemonade shocked the family into speaking to one another again. It became a guessing game of how and where in the world I came up with the makings for it.

I traded two quilt patterns, the Log Cabin Star and the Friendship Ring, with a woman back in Alton for a tiny bottle of lemon extract. She was a new bride honeymooning on the trail. She needed something to do, so she was collecting patterns to work up into a sampler.

Trying to smooth the rough trail,

Deborah

Monday evening, May 8, 1854
Independence, Missouri

Dear Betsy,

We're definitely out of the wilderness at this stop. This town, packed to the gills with people, has a colorful past. We heard about its troubled days as a Mormon metropolis in the 30's and its career as a major starting point for the Santa Fe and the California-Oregon Trails. We didn't go north to the river landing, which is several miles from town. The men want to stay south of the river.

To get out of this congestion, Albert has suggested that we cross the Blue River and go twelve miles on to Westport, on the edge of the state boundary. We'll camp our wagons and families there while the men check out the available land in this area. I have a gut feeling that Albert is not really wanting to leave Missouri.

The last two days we've run into open prairie, so there is land available in this part of Missouri. John would prefer to go on to ground that is more flat, but Albert is smitten with the area. I think the rolling land reminds Albert of the Kentucky he left behind.

Discovering that problems might follow us into Kansas has also made him consider staying in Missouri. People have been downright nosy about our beliefs as we walked across the state. They seem to sigh with relief when they hear our Southern accent, but then they ask brazenly why we don't have slaves with us. Missouri is a proslavery state and the slaveholders here are concerned about the new people coming to settle in the Kansas Territory. They want their new neighboring state to be proslavery also, to keep the harmony.

John has learned it is easiest to give a neutral response to ease the Missourians' consciences but not to commit himself one way or another to rile a temper and gun. I'm feeling uneasy as we near the border. We were just coming to Kansas for the land, not the cause. I'm beginning to wonder if we will get that choice.

James seems to be neutral about where we settle, but Mary and Nellie are urging him to look around in Missouri since Albert is hinting he'd like to stay here.

I keep thinking this was supposed to be a new family community in the territory of Kansas, but our men's opinions are starting to change the probability that we will settle together in one place.

I didn't plan to come all this way and then turn out to be completely isolated from everyone. I wish the men would think of us women and that we'd like to stay together.

Facing problems in our little camp,

Deborah

Wednesday afternoon, May 10, 1854
Westport, Missouri

Dear Betsy,

Well. . . . here we sit in camp waiting for the men to come back. The three of them left yesterday, intending to make a circle through Missouri and the Kansas Territory to scout the area. Said they would be back within a week. I think this is the longest that John and I have ever been apart. At least we women are still together.

Not the most peaceful or cleanest place to camp while we wait for the men to decide where to settle. Much to Sam's chagrin, he was left behind to take care of the camp. He would have much preferred to go with the men than be stuck with five restless women and eleven whining children. Belvard considers Sam bossy and resents his presence. I think he feels threatened because he was the "big boy" for the main part of the trip. Seems like the children have taken sides on who they want to be behind, although their loyalty seems to change daily.

Because so many people are constantly camping here, trash and filth are everywhere. People seem to forget that someone else needs the spot next. It was hard to find a halfway clean place to park the wagons. I took the shovel, racked up the garbage around our wagons, then burned it.

The Westport landing, or "City of Kansas," as it is being called, since it's on the edge of the new territory, is bustling with activity. Right on the river's edge, it is four miles north of the town of Westport. Emigrant and transport wagons dot the landscape, giving the road going through here the appearance of a river running through a huge meadow. There must be thousands of tents, wagons, and corrals of animals along the road from the town to the landing. Someone told me that 40,000 wagons left this area in '49 and '50. This is definitely a place where you can sit in one spot and watch the world go by. I hope the men can find us in this sea of wagons when they return.

A shift in the Missouri River bed a few years back caused a sandbar to form at the Independence landing, hampering steamboat docking. So, during the Mexican War, the Westport landing became the unloading point for steamboats bringing supplies for the armies. It also placed the head of the Santa Fe Trail a few miles closer to Santa Fe, and slowly the business Independence got from freighters shifted to this town and landing. Tens of thousands of men on their way to the California gold diggings poured money into this area as they started their trek across the plains. Emigrant wagon trains heading for California and the Oregon Territory followed next. This spring, the biggest group of people leaving this area is the Mormons heading for the Utah Territory.

Most of the western-bound wagon trains try to get out of here by early spring, grass permitting, so they can get across the mountains before it starts to snow. The wagon masters try to limit their groups to about twenty-five wagons so that it will be easier to keep track of everyone. The last groups of wagons are on the edge of town now, organizing to start out.

While in one store, we heard someone tell a store clerk they needed supplies for four months of travel to Oregon. Another customer spoke up, saying he made the trip in '48 and that it took their wagon train eight months to get there. The person getting outfitted waved off the grizzled-looking old man like he didn't know what he was talking about. The wife looked pensive and worried. By their clothes, you could tell they just got off a steamboat from Back East. Probably never hitched a team of oxen to a wagon before in his life, and he's ready to drag his family across the plains, desert, and mountains for an adventure.

Gigantic stockpiles of supplies and food overflow onto the boardwalks in front of the stores. The stores carry everything from barrels of every staple needed to fancy canned goods of milk, sardines, and peaches, essence of peppermint, bottles of lemon syrup, and spices I never heard of. Prices seemed three to four times higher than at home in our little store in Kentucky. Of course, the merchants have a captive audience, just getting off the boat, who need these things. You could walk in wearing a city slicker tailored suit and walk out with buckskin beeches, India rubber poncho, boots, and a frontier hat.

Down the street, a person can buy wagons at a wagon smith's. Some shops were making them out of fresh boards instead of seasoned wood, and this will cause problems for the inexperienced traveler down the road. We couldn't believe the prices they were getting for those cheap wagons.

Oxen were being sold for $50 to $75 per head. Worn out animals just getting off the trail are thin and weak and being traded for new sets. After a few weeks of rest and feed, the animals will be fit and sold again to pull another wagon going on to Oregon or Back East. Broken-down horses and unbroken mules mingle in another big corral on the edge of town. I'd hate to trade our animals, who we know so well by habit and name, off for something else, but if they were worn out, we'd have no choice. But we'd rather do that than lose an animal on the road and have nothing to replace it with.

There were enough men—some looking like I wouldn't trust my dog with them, let alone my children—hanging around the livery stables looking for jobs on the trail to help the tenderfoots. If the city people from Back East we saw in the store are smart, they would hire an honest bull whacker to guide them along the way and take care of them and their animals. Our trail has been tough along populated roads. I can't imagine what it must be like out in the wilderness.

There is also a large score of Indians hanging around the businesses and taverns. This is the closest trading place to their reservation across the border, so I hear they frequent the town. At one point, I had to remind the children not to stare when we were walking around. They haven't seen many Indians along the trail, so they are curious. I figured if the government is opening up the Kansas Territory in a few short weeks, the Indians would have already moved to the new Indian territory. Will we be displacing tepees when we buy land?

Wishing for *clean* peace and quiet,

Deborah

Dear Betsy,

We're still a little shaky, but we have everything back together as best we can. Still haven't found several things that blew away, and probably never will. John will have to fix the wagon when and if he shows up.

We haven't seen our men, so don't have any idea if they were caught in the storm. For all we know, we could be three widows stuck out on a storm-torn prairie.

Thursday was a hot sultry day without a whiff of breeze. The sky rumbled on and off for hours as if trying to make up its mind what to do. We stayed in camp and watched a thunderhead build up until it took over the entire sky. People stood by their wagons staring at the horizon, wondering what to do, for they were out in the open. The animals were antsy, milling around our makeshift corral. The dogs cowered under the wagon wheels after trying their best to jump up in the bed to hide.

With a surprising gust, the wind stirred up pockets of dust around the wagons, acting like it wasn't quite sure which way it was going to blow. Following the burst was a blast of wall-hard wind, the force like nothing I've experienced before.

Items around the campfire tossed to the flashing sky and disappeared; clothes and bedding hanging out followed. Tents and wagon covers whipped loose from their bindings, threatening to take off for the heavens. My quilt basket sitting on the wagon seat blew off and blocks of material flashed away before I could grab them. The wind was so strong we couldn't move against it.

Shouts and screams rose among the roar of the wind as several wagons toppled over in the force. Herds broke through their corrals and raced through the chaos. All at once we were in the middle of a cyclone.

I didn't know what to do, where to put six children with no stable shelter. We just huddled out in the open until pouring rain and hail drove us under a wagon. Then the bed we were under tilted, crashing into the side of the other wagon. There we stayed during the bruising storm until it finally abated.

The damage done to the camping ground was unbelievable. We stumbled among the rubble of what was left of our belongings, not knowing what to do first. Everyone was in a state of shock.

Shredded, dripping clothing hung from points of wagons, poles, and wherever else they were snagged. Cracked-open containers spilled from the overturned wagons, oozing food into the rain. One wagon near us was a smoldering ruin, having caught on fire right at first when a lit lantern blew over inside the bed. Mournful cries of the hurt slowly found our ears and senses.

I felt utterly helpless and didn't know what to do. I guess my motherly instincts took over and I checked the family first. We all had bruises and lumps on our backs and heads from hail and blowing wreckage. I think Ann sprained her wrist when her hand got caught between the spokes of a wheel when the wagon tipped over. Mary's family survived a little better since their wagons stayed upright. Sam was knocked out cold for a while when he was hit by debris while trying to stop the herd. Sallie dragged him under the wagon, which probably saved his life.

We've spent the last three days trying to find and salvage our belongings, strung over a mile-wide area with a thousand other campers' possessions. People are now bickering about who owns what since everyone had packed much the same items. Men have been on guard for looters stealing what's left.

I thank my husband's skill in carpentry in making storage boxes inside the wagon that withstood the wind's force. The bins of tools and quilts twisted but did not break open. However, the cover ripped off the other wagon and soaked our provisions. The leather sacks saved most of the food. The end gate tore loose and I lost most of my tinware. Anything light in weight disappeared.

We got the wagon righted, our possessions fairly dried out and repacked to some semblance of order. I only found a few of the quilt blocks I lost. Repaired the tears in our wagon covers and tents and did the same for other unfortunate souls.

I know of three people in our immediate vicinity who were seriously injured and two who died from wagons crushing them.

Nearly everyone has helped out if someone is lacking medicine or bandages.

There went another shot. I cringe every time I hear gunfire now. Some animals are still having to be put out of their misery because they were seriously bruised or lame. The livestock of all the campers have been contained in a big pen and owners have been trying to sort out their own stock. Sam and Belvard, luckily, found all of ours. Many people lost several head. Albert's pigs were smart and survived under the wagons. My chicken cage ripped off the wagon, did a few somersaults, and landed against another wagon. I lost one chicken and am waiting to see if the others survive. There have been no eggs since the storm. Blackie walks like he has a sore back. Tippy was protected in Robby's arms and came through without a scratch.

Battered by a prairie storm,

Deborah

Tuesday evening, May 16, 1854
Westport, Missouri

Dear Betsy,

Our men came back yesterday, unaware of last week's storm until they got a few miles within camp. Westport had a few broken windows when they came through town, but no other damage. I guess the storm was worse around the river.

They couldn't believe what a mess we told them this place was five days ago, because the camping ground has been cleaned up. Most campers burned what they couldn't salvage and moved on to where they were headed. New wagons rolled in while we waited for our husbands to come back.

Repairs were made on the wagons and supplies bought in town to restock what we had lost and needed to move on. The money bills in my waist pocket have dwindled faster than we had planned for this trip. We head on with a very limited reserve, considering we still need to buy land.

John came back with his jaw set and a tense look in his eye. The three of them couldn't decide on one place to settle. They made a loop west following the Kansas River into the new territory about sixty miles until they ran out of trees, then cut down south to the Pottawatomie Creek. Then they rode back to Westport, zigzagging through the Missouri counties to see what was still available there.

James and Albert have picked out land in Cass County, Missouri, although not next to each other. Sounds like they'll be about a day's ride apart.

John is still determined to go to Kansas. He said the best-looking farmland he's ever seen is just beyond the Shawnee reservation. I couldn't talk him into moving down to Cass County to wait until the territory is officially open by the government. He's not going to wait on the border while floods of people rush in early to stake the best land.

Gossip in the Westport stores is his other argument to move to Kansas in haste. John heard that cholera is turning up in the towns on the Mississippi River and heading west through the Missouri Valley.

I'll send this letter off tomorrow as we go through Westport. John plans to get back on the road west into Kansas. We'll see where that leads us. I have no idea when I'll get able to send a letter saying where we have settled.

Tomorrow I'll have to say goodbye to the last of our family. We'll miss strong Mary and industrious Nellie. They helped Ann and me out so much on the trip. I pray we settle near the border so we can still visit them once a year or so. We four women have been through quite a bit on our two-month trip from Kentucky. I assume they will write back to Kentucky to say where they have settled.

Just for your peace of mind, you should know your grand-children all sport rosy faces and have grown over an inch each since we left. I'm proud of how the boys took responsibility on this journey. It's been a hard task for ones so young.

Sarah and George Ann were greatly disappointed but yet happy that Tippy found his former owners. Just by chance they were camped here too during the storm and spotted him while looking for their strewn belongings. There was no doubt, when Tippy heard the voice of the little boy, who he really belonged to. While in Westport getting the last of our provisions, I asked around and found two kittens for the girls. I hope it will help make up for the lost of their five cousins and playmates.

John, as you can guess, is still hale, hearty, and stubborn as ever. Ann's health has improved a little with the warm prairie weather, and she looks forward to quilting her wedding quilt.

I'm still healthy in body, but weary and restless in spirit. I won't feel safe until we have a roof over our family's head and food in a cellar. There is still a wary feeling in my mind about trouble ahead in Kansas that I can't shake. I hope that after seeing our land, my fears will disappear.

I hope this letter finds you well. I miss you greatly and wish you were here with us.

Resigned to my destiny,

Deborah

Jumping the Gun

Friday evening, May 19, 1854
on our land in Kansas

Dear Betsy,

Against my better judgement, we left Westport and our family on Wednesday. I did not bid them farewell, because then I would feel like I would never see them again. I felt almost as bad as when I left family in Kentucky. There was this dreadful feeling in the back of my mind that we shouldn't part with James and Mary. Maybe it was because we had become so close, and depended on one another during our journey. And I must admit, I felt a little ashamed because I secretly felt that if we hadn't stopped in Boone County to get the Tiptons, John's brother and family would still be with us. I hope we can at least exchange letters to find out where we've all settled.

We stuck to the road that follows the south side of the meandering Kansas River. The trail cuts through the Shawnee Indian lands. It was a very eerie feeling to have silent Indians watching us go by. I felt like we were trespassing straight through their farmyard, which in a sense I guess we were.

I felt more at ease with the Indians after we took a morning break by the Shawnee Baptist Mission. We visited with the missionary family who runs the school for the Shawnee children and found out the Indians on the reservation have been civilized for years. I believe the man said there were about 900 people living on this reservation. Many live in houses and farms just like we do. The little Indian children, dressed in ordinary clothes like ours, were outside for recess and invited our brood to round out their numbers for a game. These children probably have a better education than my own.

I must say we crossed beautiful country here, so green and lush it looks good enough to eat. The prairie rolls gently up and down to creeks that are edged by good stands of oak, elm, hickory, and walnut. And they are good-sized timbers that are large enough to use now instead of little saplings, like we've seen along some waters. The fragrance of wild plum blossoms, so thick on the edge of the creeks, is overpowering. Intermixed with the prairie grass, we spied spring flowers of purple, white, and yellow, different types than what we had in Kentucky. Wildlife is so abundant that we scared up a prairie grouse or rabbit almost every mile.

We camped on the edge of a little side creek the first evening. It was a warm night, with a slight breeze drifting through our camp. The children spent the evening trying to catch the first fireflies we've seen on the trip and dodge mosquitoes at the same time. I lit a buffalo chip in a pail and smoked the mosquitoes out of our tent before we went to bed. I think I slept better than any night we spent in Westport, probably because John was back safe with us.

We were not alone on the vast prairie, though. Many people, mostly Missourians, are jumping the gun also to get first shot at the best land in Kansas. People from the neighboring state have heard that groups from the North are headed this way to make Kansas a free state and to start an underground railroad to help the Missouri slaves escape. I don't think the Missourians plan to move, just mark the land along the border so no one from the North can stake a claim there.

We've had no problems with these campers since we have a southern drawl. I guess they figure we're just too poor right now to own slaves since we look so ragged and worn out.

Last night we camped near Pascal Fish's Hotel. He's an Indian who has run a tavern, hotel, and trading post for years. People going west to California on this road are keeping him prosperous. Happy to talk to travelers, he told us about the strange abrupt hill, called Blue Mound, that we had been seeing for miles in the distant gray-blue haze. Mr. Fish told us the legend that Indian maidens wept tears from the hilltop when their warriors didn't return from battle. Their stream of tears formed the Wakarusa and Kansas Rivers.

Today we followed the road two miles until it crossed the Wakarusa River that the Indian talked about. After crossing, John decided to veer off the road and follow the stream west a ways. The Wakarusa is a fine stream of clear water, between a creek and a river in size, with heavy timber on its banks. John thought it is big enough that it shouldn't dry up in the summer.

After traveling about three miles, John stopped. It was like he had been guided to this place on earth and knew exactly where to settle. After the problems of farming Kentucky's hills, John wanted the flattest farm land he could find, and this was it. Rolling prairie surrounds the Wakarusa River Valley, but not on this acreage. I'd say we ended up about forty miles west of Westport.

I wish you could have seen how he looked. John's tired shoulders lifted and his face beamed with satisfaction. This was going to be his land. At this point I looked hard at our surroundings. Our trip was over and this was going to be my home for the rest of my life. Suddenly, I felt exhausted. My family had survived the trip and I could finally rest.

Well, that thought lasted two seconds until I realized I needed to start the noon meal. Then it dawned on me how much work we have to do! We can't camp forever. We have no home, no furniture, no food to harvest, no shelter for the animals. Our first task will be getting an acreage of sod plowed so we can get grains and vegetables planted immediately. We don't know how long the growing season is here, but we need to have food grown and harvested before the snow flies.

We'll live in the tent while we get a shelter built. We've passed dugouts and soddies through Missouri. I'm not sure if we'll use that method or cut timber from the river for a log house. I'm sure winters are worse here than in Kentucky, but how bad, and how long do they last? I guess we'll be experiencing it firsthand.

John walked and measured out the 160 acres we wanted to claim so he could mark the corners with stakes bearing his name.

He put part of our acreage on both sides of the river to protect our water rights. Of course these are just rough estimates since the state hasn't been surveyed yet. Our boundary line will likely change. We'll put our house along the river in the middle of the claim. I hope we won't have to move it.

Three horsemen are sharing our fire tonight. John was uneasy at first when the men rode up midafternoon. They ended up helping him mark the land and unload a wagon instead of jumping the claim. They are from Illinois, Ohio originally, and were traveling through the new territory to check out the land. After seeing the Wakarusa River Valley, they have decided to bring their families back here to settle. Sounds like it will be a big wagon train, with family and friends traveling together. The one young man, a Will Kennedy, said that he thinks at least seven of his siblings will relocate their families here. A Mr. Holloway with him was a brother-in-law, and the other man, a John Wood, was a friend. Kennedy's widowed mother is still in Ohio but plans to bring his younger siblings to Illinois to make the trip with them. If the families all get along with one another and stake claims together, they will fill up the valley by themselves.

I'm finishing the letter tonight because the trio offered to mail the letter for me when they pass through Westport on their way home. Considering they were Northern men, we hit it off with them immediately. I wouldn't mind having them as neighbors.

I just realized that this letter finishes my saga of the trail to you. We've traveled about 750 miles in 66 days, across five states. We've seen all kinds of terrain, towns, and people, been in every type of weather imaginable, and all arrived at our destination safe and sound.

Finally at our trail's end,

Deborah

Thursday evening, August 17, 1854
on our land in Kansas

Dear Betsy,

I'm sorry I haven't written since May. There is so much work to do this summer—it has been overwhelming at times. I realized it would have been your wedding anniversary today with Father, so I thought I'd write you a letter. I'll send Belvard to Fish's Hotel with the letter tomorrow so it can catch the stagecoach to West-port to be mailed.

The Kansas prairie has changed dramatically around us when I think of how I described it in your last letter. The prairie grass is showing the slightest tint of golden-red along the tall stems. Our crops are a healthy, dark green. The worn-out animals are fat and sleek again. Temperatures are hot and humid, not much different than Kentucky really, except we're more out in the open here. Blowing wind is a daily given. Rain has been sporadic or heavy at times. At least we aren't having a dry summer like they are Back East.

After weeks of wondering if we would get to stay on our land, we finally got word that the Territory of Kansas bill was passed by the government. It was such a relief that we could finally, legally claim the land we picked out. John and his gun have had to run off so many claim jumpers that I've lost count. That problem has dropped considerably now that we have a crop growing and it looks like someone lives on this land. We're definitely not the only ones here in Kansas!

Our oxen and plow started turning sod the day after we got here. John kept plowing practically day and night while the boys planted the grain seed. The soil here has a deep top layer of a dark rich loam that has already yielded larger corn plants than we would have in Kentucky by this time of summer, even with the late planting. Mr. Fish said to expect 25 to 100 bushels of corn per acre. And we were happy to get a few bushels per acre on our Kentucky farm. We also planted oats and sorghum that we hope yields as well.

The garden seeds that traveled with us are producing a healthy patch of vegetables. It was a celebration when we picked and cooked the first green beans. It has been heaven to have fresh food again. And we'll have potatoes, pumpkins, carrots, onions, and turnips to store for this winter. Some of my uneasiness about our trip has abated since we have food for this winter now.

Children are all busy helping out with the homesteading. The boys have spent many hours planting and hoeing in the new fields, building fences and cutting down trees for the house. The girls are in charge of pulling weeds and harvesting the garden. While exploring the area they have found wild fruit along the river. We've already picked and dried plums, currants, mulberries, and grapes. We have our eye on walnuts and honey to harvest this fall.

The process of building our log house has started. After the fields were plowed and planted, John and the boys cut trees from along the river, dragged them to where our house will be built, and trimmed the branches off. The logs need to dry and cure before they are stacked into walls. In the meantime, the ends need to be notched with the axe to get them to fit together. The plan is to get it built next month before we start to harvest the crops.

For now, we're living in a hay tent. John needed one of the wagons unloaded, and we needed a place to store our belongings and supplies. All those things and all of us did not fit in our little tent, so we built a temporary shelter. Many people around here have put up an A-frame of ridgepoles, layered it with limbs, thatched it with tall prairie grass on the sides, and are calling it home, just like us. I do not plan to live in it this winter, though. A person would freeze to death. The hay tent only keeps you halfway dry and out of the wind.

Ann is anxious to get the house done so we can put up the quilting frame and commence on her quilt. She has had such an urgency to get it done that it's been vexing at times. No, she does not have a man calling on her, although there are plenty around. To get started, we talked about setting up the frame outside in a week or two when the weather cools off. I'm afraid our sweaty hands would dirty her fine top right now. I realize it will take longer to quilt, for neighboring women are few and far between at this point. I keep telling her she has all winter to quilt. I do have my Friendship blocks to put together, but I need to repair and make winter clothing for the children first.

Towns are cropping up everywhere. Large groups of people are filtering in faster than we can keep track. Some of the towns are just paper, meaning they are plotted and advertised, but no actual buildings are in place if you go to the land where the town is supposed to be. Two of these towns look like they will make it and thrive.

A group of about thirty men from Back East, calling themselves the New England Emigrant Aid Society, have set up a tent town called Lawrence about four miles northwest of us. They say another group of two hundred, consisting of families this time, is on their way to join them. This is the first united group of Northerners against slavery that have settled in this area.

In contrast, there is another town, Franklin, two miles northeast of us that is full of proslavery believers. I'm guessing over 100 people, mostly men, are living in every type of shelter imaginable and starting to build houses in town. A sawmill has been put up to cut lumber from the tree stands around the area.

We see claim marks everywhere we go, but very few real houses with families on them. Most were staked, and maybe part of a house was built to make it look like a homestead is in progress, but in most cases the squatter went back home to Missouri.

We are trying to stay neutral between the two sides. I hope problems don't arise as more people move to the area.

Making a home in Kansas,

Deborah

Tuesday, February 6, 1855
homestead on the Wakarusa River

Dear Betsy,

It's a cold, rainy day here in Kansas. The drizzle, fog, and dampness remind me of the day we left Kentucky last March. My mood is about the same, too. Huddled by the fire, I have sat here a long time with the pen in my hand, trying to form the words I need to put down on paper.

I'm afraid this letter brings sad news. I've put off writing for a week, but I need to let you know about Ann. She finally succumbed to consumption and passed away on Wednesday, January 30. Her condition kept weakening over the fall, and she was bedridden by Christmas. I regret not letting you know sooner that she was gravely ill, but Ann made me promise I would not write to you about her situation. There was nothing you could do for her, being so far away, and she didn't want you to start mourning her inevitable death.

Her passing has left a terrible hole in our lives. We didn't realize how much we depended on her until she wasn't there to make cookies or wipe a runny nose. She's been an extra mother to my children and I think that eased her pain that she never had the chance to marry and raise a family of her own.

She worked feverishly on her wedding quilt until it was done. That quilt became an obsession and kept her alive longer than I expected. When it was finished, her condition deteriorated rapidly. I could not stand the thought of her being in the frozen ground alone, so we buried her in the quilt. Ann loved to sit on the edge of the stream that runs through our place, so she's buried on the bank of the Wakarusa.

I do want to assure you that all of us have survived the winter so far and don't show any signs of catching Ann's disease.

I miss her terribly, Betsy. I was her big sister and I should have taken better care of her. She would be alive today if we hadn't talked her into going to Kansas with us. Looking back, I know the trip was a strain on her health, not a help for it.

Ann was the quiet salvation that kept me sane on the trail. She lightened the load of cooking and washing so I could take better care of my children. Maybe her mission in life was to safely see me and my family to Kansas. I hope my angel Ann continues to watch over us.

You know I worried about not being buried in Kentucky with family. Now Ann will be here waiting for me when it is my turn to die.

After Ann's funeral, I put a small Sister's Choice quilt top into the quilting frame. After Ann finished her Rose of Sharon, she starting piecing this little quilt because I'm expecting another child this summer. It was Ann's way of being part of the next child's life, even though she knew she would never see it grow up. She never got to quilt it together.

When the baby arrives, I'll wrap it in Ann's quilt and tell him or her about our trail to Kansas and how a special woman helped us get here.

Finishing Ann's final trail of thread,

Deborah

Pine Tree

Memory Block

Rose of Sharon

Mountain Lily

Slave Chain

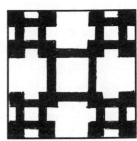

Sassafras Leaf

Dutchman's Puzzle

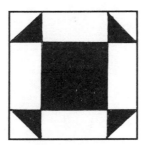

Kitty-Corner

Log Cabin Star

Friendship Ring

Indiana Puzzle

Sister's Choice

Family Chart

John Pieratt (1817-1868)
Deborah (Goodpaster) Pieratt (1821-1859)

children:
1. Levi (1840-1840)
2. Belvard (1841-1870)
3. James Monroe (1844-1913)
4. Robert Letcher (1846-1863)
5. Sarah (1848-1903)
6. George Ann (1850-1879)
7. Emma (1854-1929)
8. John Franklin (1855-1908)

James Pieratt (1818-1888)
Mary (Tipton) Pieratt (1815-1903)

children:
1. James Samuel (1846-1917)
2. Albert Worth (1848-1926)
3. William Butler (1849-1904)
4. John Monroe (1851-1899)
5. Valentine Letcher (1853-1901)

Albert Tipton (1808-dec.)
Sallie (Tipton) Tipton (1815-dec.)

child:
1. Samuel Barnett (1835-1869)

Other family members on trip

Ann Goodpaster, Deborah's sister (1824-1855)
Nellie Tipton, Mary and Albert's sister (1807-dec.)

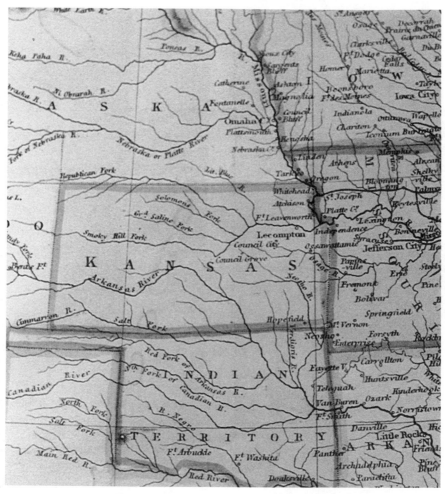

States crossed on trip (1845 map)

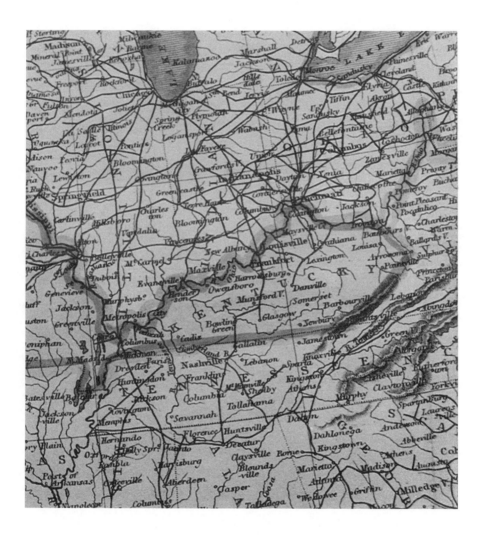

103

Bibliography

Andreas, A. T. *History of the State of Kansas.* Chicago: A. T. Andreas, 1883.

Angle, Paul M. *Prairie State: Impressions of Illinois, 1673-1967, by Travelers and Other Observers.* Chicago: The University of Chicago Press, 1968.

The Annals of America, Volume 8, 1850-1857. Chicago: Encyclopaedia Britannica, Inc, 1968.

Bailey, Thomas A. *The American Pageant: A History of the Republic.* Boston: D. C. Heath and Company, 1961.

Bloch, Louis M., Jr., ed. *Overland to California in 1859.* Cleveland: Bloch and Company, 1984.

Botkin, B. A. *A Treasury of Western Folklore.* New York: Bonanza Books, 1975.

Brewerton, George D. *In the Buffalo Country.* Ashland, Ore.: Lewis Osborne, 1970.

Butruille, Susan G. *Women's Voices from the Oregon Trail.* Boise, Idaho: Tamarack Books, Inc., 1993.

Channing, Steven A. *Kentucky.* New York: W. W. Norton & Company, Inc., 1977.

Clark, Thomas D. *Kentucky: Land of Contrast.* New York: Harper & Row, 1968.

Clarke, Dwight L. *The Original Journals of Henry Smith Turner.* Norman: University of Oklahoma Press, 1966.

Combined History of Edwards, Lawrence and Wabash County, Illinois. Philadelphia: J. L. McDonough & Co., 1883.

Connelley, William Elsey. *A Standard History of Kansas and Kansans, Volume 1*. Chicago: Lewis Publishing Co., 1918.

Cooper, Frank A. *It Happened in Kansas*. 4 Vols. Lyons, Kans.: Velma Cooper Purdy, 1991.

Dary, David. *True Tales of the Old-Time Plains*. New York: Crown Publishers, Inc., 1979.

Davis, Carolyn O'Bagy. *Pioneer Quiltmaker: The Story of Dorinda Moody Slade, 1808-1895*. Tucson, Ariz.: Sanpete Publications, 1990.

————. *Quilted All Day: The Prairie Journals of Ida Chambers Melugin*. Tucson, Ariz.: Sanpete Publications, 1993.

Dick, Everett. *The Sod-House Frontier, 1854-1890*. Lincoln, Neb.: Johnsen Publishing Company, 1954.

Drago, Harry Sinclair. *Roads to Empire*. New York: Dodd, Mead & Company, 1968.

Everton, George B., Jr., ed. *The Handy Book for Genealogists*. Logan, Utah: The Everton Publishers, Inc., 1994.

Feltskog, E. N., ed. *The Oregon Trail*. Madison: The University of Wisconsin Press, 1969.

Gleed, Charles S., ed. *The Kansas Memorial: A Report of the Old Settlers' Meetings held at Bismarck Grove, Kansas, September 15 and 16, 1879*. Kansas City, Mo.: Press of Ramsey, Millett and Hudson, 1880.

Goodrich, DeWitt C., and Charles R. Tuttle. *An Illustrational History of the State of Indiana*. Indianapolis: Richard S. Peale & Co., 1875.

Greeley, Horace. *An Overland Journey from New York to San Francisco in the Summer of 1859*. New York: Alfred A. Knopf, Inc., 1864.

Haggart, Virginia, and Dorothy Harvey, eds. *My Folks Claimed the Plains*. Topeka, Kan.: Stauffer Publications, Inc., 1978.

Hall, Carrie A., and Rose G. Kretsinger. *The Romance of the Patchwork Quilt in America*. Caldwell, Idaho: The Caxton Printers, 1935.

106

Hams, Betty. *Missouri's Early Home Remedies*. Sioux City, Iowa: Quixote Press, 1992.

Hart, A. B. *The American Nation: A History. Vol. XVI, Slavery and Abolition, 1831-1841*. New York: Harper & Brothers Publishers, 1906.

Hill, William E. *The Oregon Trail: Yesterday and Today*. Caldwell, Idaho: The Caxton Printers, 1987.

History of Boone County, Missouri. St. Louis: Western Historical Co., 1821.

The History of Brown County, Ohio. Chicago: W. H. Beer and Company, 1883.

History of St. Claire County, Illinois. Philadelphia: Brink, McDonough & Co., 1881.

History of Cass and Bates County, Missouri. St. Joseph, Mo.: National Historical Co., 1883.

Holmes, Kenneth L., ed. *Covered Wagon Women: Diaries and Letters from the Western Trails, 1840-1890*. Glendale, Calif.: Arthur H. Clark Co., 1983.

Howard, Robert P. *Illinois: A History of the Prairie State*. Grand Rapids, Mich.: William B. Erdmans Publishing Company, 1972.

Huff, Alta Maxwell, and Louise Fowler Roote, eds. *My Folks Came in a Covered Wagon*. Topeka, Kan.: Stauffer Publications, Inc., 1976.

Jensen, Richard J. *Illinois*. New York: W. W. Norton & Company, Inc., 1978.

Josephy, Alvin M., Jr. *The American Heritage History of The Great West*. New York: American Heritage Publishing Co., 1965.

Lee, Wayne C., and Howard C. Raynesford. *Trails of the Smoky Hill*. Caldwell, Idaho: The Caxton Printers, 1980.

Levine, Ellen. *...If You Traveled West in a Covered Wagon*. New York: Scholastic, Inc., 1992.

Lienhard, Heinrich. *From St. Louis to Sutter's Fort, 1846*. Norman: University of Oklahoma Press, 1961.

Luchetti, Cathy. *Home on the Range: A Culinary History of the American West.* New York: Villard Books, 1993.

Marcy, Randolph B. *The Prairie Traveler: A Handbook for Overland Expeditions.* New York: Harper & Brothers, Publishers, 1859.

McReynolds, Edwin C. *Missouri: A History of the Crossroads State.* Norman: University of Oklahoma Press, 1962.

Miner, Craig. *West of Wichita.* Lawrence: University Press of Kansas, 1986.

Moody, Ralph. *The Old Trails West.* New York: Thomas Y. Crowell Company, 1963.

Morgan, Dale, ed. *Overland In 1846: Diaries and Letters of the California-Oregon Trail, Vos. I and II.* Georgetown, Calif.: The Talisman Press, 1963.

Mott, Frank Luther. *Missouri Reader.* Columbus: University of Missouri Press, 1964.

Oliva, Leo E. *Soldiers on the Santa Fe Trail.* Norman: University of Oklahoma Press, 1967.

Orlofsky, Patsy, and Myron Orlofsky. *Quilts in America.* New York: Abbeville Press, Inc., 1992.

Orpen, Adela E. *Memories of the Old Emigrant Days in Kansas, 1862-1865.* New York: Harper & Brothers Publishers, 1928.

Parkman, Francis, Jr. *The Oregon Trail.* New York: Penguin Books, 1982.

Pickham, Howard H. *Indiana.* New York: W. W. Norton & Company, Inc., 1978.

Pigney, Joseph. *For Fear We Shall Perish.* New York: E. P. Dutton & Co., Inc., 1961.

Riley, Glenda. *The Female Frontier.* Lawrence: University Press of Kansas, 1988.

Ross, Nancy Wilson. *Westward the Women.* San Francisco: North Point Press, 1985.

Ruth, Kent. *Great Day in the West: Forts, Posts, and Rendezvous Beyond the Mississippi.* Norman: University of Oklahoma Press, 1963.

Schlissel, Lillian. *Women's Diaries of the Westward Journey.* New York: Schocken Books, 1982.

Simmons, Marc. *Following the Santa Fe Trail.* Santa Fe, New Mex.: Ancient City Press, 1984.

Smith, Theodore Clarke. *The American Nation: A History. Vol. XVIII, Parties and Slavery, 1850-1859.* New York: Harper & Brothers Publishers, 1906.

Stewart, George R. *The California Trail.* Lincoln: University of Nebraska Press, 1962.

Streeter, Floyd Benjamin. *The Kaw: The Heart of a Nation.* New York: Farrar & Rinehart, 1941.

Sunder, John E., ed. *Matt Field on the Santa Fe Trail.* Norman: University of Oklahoma Press, 1960.

Thompson, Carl N., comp. *Historical Collections of Brown County, Ohio.* Ripley, Ohio: n.p., 1969.

Underwood, Larry D. *Love and Glory: Women of the Old West.* Lincoln: Media Publishing, 1991.

Unruh, John D., Jr. *The Plains Across.* Chicago: University of Illinois Press, 1979.

U.S. Government Records, county and state, for Kentucky, Indiana, Illinois, Missouri, and Kansas.

Walton, George. *Sentinel of the Plains: Fort Leavenworth and the American West.* Englewood Cliffs, New Jer.: Prentice-Hall, Inc., 1973.

Wilder, Laura Ingalls. *On the Way Home.* New York: Harper & Row, 1962.

Williams, Jacqueline. *Wagon Wheel Kitchens: Food on the Oregon Trail.* Lawrence: University Press of Kansas, 1993.

Worchester, Don, ed. *Pioneer Trails West.* Caldwell, Idaho: The Western Writers of America, 1985.

Planting Dreams Series

Drought has scorched the farmland of Sweden and there is no harvest to feed families or livestock. Taxes are due and there is little money to pay them.

But there is a ship sailing for America, where the government is giving land to anyone who wants to claim a homestead.

So begins a migration out of Sweden to a new life on the Great Plains of America.

Can you imagine starting a journey to an unknown country, not knowing what the country would be like, where you would live, or how you would survive? Did you make the right decision to leave in the first place?

Planting Dreams
Follow Charlotta Johnson and her family as they travel by ship and rail from their homeland in 1868, to their homestead on the open plains of Kansas.
Quality soft book • $9.95 • ISBN 1-886652-11-2
6 x 9 • 124 pages

Cultivating Hope
Through hardship and heartache Charlotta and Samuel face crises with their children and their land as they build their farmstead.
Quality soft book • $9.95 • ISBN 1-886652-12-0
6 x 9 • 124 pages

Harvesting Faith
The work and sacrifice of the family's first years on the prairie are reaped in the growth of the family, farm and community.
Quality soft book • $9.95 • ISBN 1-886652-13-9
6 x 9 • 124 pages

Books by Linda K. Hubalek

the *Butter in the Well* series

Butter in the Well

Read the endearing account of Kajsa Svensson Runeberg, an immigrant wife who recounts how she and
her family built up a farm on the unsettled prairie.
Quality soft book • $9.95 • ISBN 1-886652-00-7
6 x 9 • 144 pages

Prärieblomman

This tender, touching diary continues the saga of
Kajsa Runeberg's family through her daughter,
Alma, as she blossoms into a young woman.
Quality soft book • $9.95 • ISBN 1-886652-01-5
6 x 9 • 144 pages
Abr. audio cassette • $9.95 • ISBN 1-886652-05-8
90 minutes

Egg Gravy

Everyone who's ever treasured a family recipe or
marveled at the special touches Mother added to her
cooking will enjoy this collection of recipes and wisdom from the homestead family.
Quality soft book • $9.95 • ISBN 1-886652-02-3
6 x 9 • 136 pages

Looking Back

During her final week on the land she homesteaded,
Kajsa reminisces about the growth and changes she
experienced during her 51 years on the farm. Don't
miss this heart-touching finale!
Quality soft book • $9.95 • ISBN 1-886652-03-1
6 x 9 • 140 pages

(continued on next page)

Butter in the Well **note cards**— Three full-color designs per package, featuring the family and farm.

Homestead **note cards**—This full-color design shows the original homestead.

Either style of note card —$4.95/ set. Each set contains 6 cards and envelopes in a clear vinyl pouch. Each card: 5 1/2 x 4 1/4 inches.

Postcards— One full-color design of homestead. $3.95 for a packet of 12.

the *Trail of Thread series*

Trail of Thread
Taste the dust of the road and feel the wind in your face as you travel with a Kentucky family by wagon trail to the new territory of Kansas in 1854.

Quality soft book • $9.95 • ISBN 1-886652-06-6
6 x 9 • 124 pages

Thimble of Soil
Experience the terror of the fighting and the determination to endure as you stake a claim alongside the women caught in the bloody conflicts of Kansas in the 1850s.

Quality soft book • $9.95 • ISBN 1-886652-07-4
6 x 9 • 120 pages

Stitch of Courage
Face the uncertainty of the conflict and challenge the purpose of the fight with the women of Kansas during the Civil War.
Quality soft book • $9.95 • ISBN 1-886652-08-2
6 x 9 • 120 pages

Order Form

Butterfield Books, Inc.
P.O. Box 407
Lindsborg, KS 67456-0407
1-800-790-2665 / 785-227-2707 / 785-227-2017, fax
www.butterfieldbooks.com

SEND TO:

Name _____

Address _____

City _____

State _____ Zip _____

Phone # _____

❏ Check enclosed for entire amount payable to

Butterfield Books

❏ Visa ❏ MasterCard ❏ Discover

Card # ☐☐☐☐ ☐☐☐☐ ☐☐☐☐ ☐☐☐☐

Exp Date ☐☐

Signature (or call to place your order) _____ Date _____

ISBN #	TITLE	QTY	UNIT PRICE	TOTAL
1-886652-00-7	Butter in the Well		9.95	
1-886652-01-5	Prarieblomman		9.95	
1-886652-02-3	Egg Gravy		9.95	
1-886652-03-1	Looking Back		9.95	
	Butter in the Well Series - 4 books		35.95	
1-886652-05-8	**Cassette:** Prarieblomman		9.95	
	Note Cards: Butter in the Well		4.95	
	Note Cards: Homestead		4.95	
	Postcards: Homestead		3.95	
1-886652-06-6	Trail of Thread		9.95	
1-886652-07-4	Thimble of Soil		9.95	
1-886652-08-2	Stitch of Courage		9.95	
	Trail of Thread Series - 3 books		26.95	
1-886652-11-2	Planting Dreams		9.95	
1-886652-12-0	Cultivating Hope		9.95	
1-886652-13-9	Harvesting Faith		9.95	
	Planting Dreams Series - 3 books		26.95	
			Subtotal	
			KS add 7.3% tax	
Shipping & Handling: per address ($3.00 for 1st book. Each add'l. book .50)				
			Total	

Retailers and Libraries: Books are available through Butterfield Books, Baker & Taylor, Bergquist Imports, Booksource, Checker Distributors, Ingram, Skandisk and Western International.

RIF Programs and Schools: Contact Butterfield Books for discount, ordering and author appearances.